The Triumph of Artificial Intelligence

Günter Cisek

The Triumph of Artificial Intelligence

How Artificial Intelligence is Changing the Way We Live Together

 Springer

Günter Cisek
Würzburg, Germany

ISBN 978-3-658-34898-4   ISBN 978-3-658-34896-0 (eBook)
https://doi.org/10.1007/978-3-658-34896-0

This book is a translation of the original German edition "Machtwechsel der Intelligenzen" by Cisek, Günter, published by Springer Fachmedien Wiesbaden GmbH in 2021. The translation was done with the help of artificial intelligence (machine translation by the service DeepL.com). A subsequent human revision was done primarily in terms of content, so that the book will read stylistically differently from a conventional translation. Springer Nature works continuously to further the development of tools for the production of books and on the related technologies to support the authors.

This Springer imprint is published by the registered company Springer Fachmedien Wiesbaden GmbH part of Springer Nature.
The registered company address is: Abraham-Lincoln-Str. 46, 65189 Wiesbaden, Germany

For my glorious grandchildren, that I wish, that they will be part of the first generation of Immortals
. . .

Preface

The author is constantly surprised by how little politicians and executives seriously care about artificial intelligence (AI), even though it is quite obvious that AI will dramatically change all areas of life in the near future. Therefore, this book aims to enable social and commercial decision-makers, but also any interested reader, to no longer meet AI experts with a lack of knowledge or "black-box" phobia, but as a savvy "customer" who knows the real possibilities but also the typical problems and current limitations of AI and proactively helps to determine its use.

Therefore, the explanations are not limited to the fields of application of AI, but in Chaps. 2 and 3 the necessary technical prerequisites are also described in detail, so that the reader is also given access to the "inner life" of AI and thus becomes aware of the possibilities and limitations of AI.

Nevertheless, the manifold application areas of AI are of course illustrated in detail in order to give the AI user or affected person suggestions as to how he can use this new intelligence to make life easier. The fact that the last two chapters also contain a bit of speculation and philosophizing is a real challenge for the topic and hopefully increases the reading pleasure.

Würzburg, Germany
September 2020

Günter Cisek

Acknowledgements

In the process of writing this book, unexpected and completely surprising consternation on the subject of "artificial intelligence" occurred to the author, for which I am very grateful.

For bringing this book to fruition, I have a great many kind people to thank, who motivated me to produce a layman's understandable yet detailed account of the subject. You may forgive me if I mention only a few of you personally in my acknowledgements.

First and foremost among them is Prof. Dr. Med. Gay, who with his always encouraging feedback made it very enjoyable for me to continue writing. I also remember with pleasure the stimulating discourses on singularity with General Music Director E. Calesso. I am very grateful to Mr. Steffen Höfner, M.Sc., who supported me considerably in the description of the techniques. My thanks also go to his wife Bettina Höfner, the Germanist, who meticulously worked through my manuscript for stylistic and orthographic errors. Substantial input was provided by my son Dr. Robert Cisek with his rich practical experience in the chapter on Industry 4.0. My daughter Dr. D. Schönbeck is to thank for the apt title of the book. Last but not least, I would also like to thank my dear wife, who patiently allowed me the time for research and writing and thereby benevolently compensated for the neglect of my domestic duties.

I am also indebted to Springer Verlag. Chief editor Petra Steinmüller supervised the creation of the book with caring cordiality, and Ms Sophia Leonhard was always a very reliable and professional support to me as an editor.

Contents

How Much and What Kind of Artificial Intelligence Can Humans Bear?

The science that is done today is the magic mirror into which we have to look if we want to catch a glimpse of what is to come. (Y. Gasset)

Fritz put the expensive contact lenses back in the case, shooked out his arms and snuggled up to the warming fireplace. He had just completed a virtual flight over Cologne's old town as a pigeon. A sharp wind had blown around his beak above the cathedral spires, so that he was still shivering now. He had to smile at himself: despite being fully aware that it had only been a fictional experience in virtual space, his body had reacted psychosomatically as if he had been buzzing around above the Altstadt for real. "Maybe the dualists should give this phenomenon some thought," he mused as he rubbed his ice-cold feet.

While Dr. Weishaupt was still desperately trying to free himself from inside the car, a police patrol was already racing up. And Mr. Winterbrot had to apologise profusely to both the police and Dr. Weishaupt. He had forgotten to switch off the sensor system when he had proudly invited his colleague on the board to try out the comfort of his new premium class company car. He had already installed the new Koshimizu seat with its 360 sensors, which assigns a load index from 0 to 265 to each point and, using the code calculated from this, immediately recognises any butt stored in the seat. Dr. Weishaupt had not yet been scanned, of course, and was thus immediately reported to the police as a car thief in the "Internet of Things" (IoT).

After 40 years Günter entered his then frequently visited favourite pub "The Victoria" with fond memories of his student days at the LSE. Nothing had changed. And it was still as 'crowded' as it had been back then. As he tried to squeeze his way to the bar, the charming bartender was already asking him over the heads of the other patrons what he would like to drink, and a little later he already had his beloved Pale Ale in his hand. He

© Springer Fachmedien Wiesbaden GmbH, part of Springer Nature 2021
G. Cisek, *The Triumph of Artificial Intelligence*,
https://doi.org/10.1007/978-3-658-34896-0_1

was completely amazed at the quick service and secretly admired the amazing overview of the lady behind the counter in the so overflowing pub. Günter, of course, did not know that when he entered, his face had already been scanned and given a cardinal number. That's why, as he only now noticed, there was no jostling, because the regulars of course knew that here with the service it was exactly "one after the other".

If some readers now believe that they have accidentally "downloaded" a science fiction book, the author can reassure them. The three anecdotes described here are not science fiction, but real examples of the so-called "weak AI" or "artificial narrow intelligence"(**ANI** for Artificial Narrow Intelligence). It's hard to imagine what would happen in the pub if the "strong AI" or Artificial Super Intelligence (**ASI**) had already established itself there. Probably then frightened cyborgs would inject some ominous molecular cocktails between the synapses of sheer disembodied neutron sponges.—Don't worry, most experts expect a functioning strong AI by 2045 at the earliest.[1]

The definition of "artificial intelligence" is difficult because the term itself is controversial, especially since there is no consensus among intelligence researchers on the nature of "intelligence". Among other things, the ability to reason, logic, planning, emotional knowledge, consciousness, creativity, problem solving, judgement and learning are subsumed under this term.[2] With these characteristics the classical intelligence concept of the 1970s is probably rather characterized, on which also the intelligence test from the psychological diagnostics is based. In the meantime one speaks additionally of completely new human intelligences such as emotional, social, musical-rhythmic, physical-kinesthetic[3] (!) and even spiritual or extraterrestrial (SETI = Search for Exterrestrial Intelligence) intelligence.[4] To the author this term seems to be a bit overused, because if with "inter" = "between" and "legere" = "to recognize, to understand" the cognitive ability is meant, one wonders at least how one can be physically or spiritually "intelligent".

At least Tegmark offers a concise definition: "Intelligence = The ability to achieve complex goals."[5] Accordingly, syllogistically concluded, "Artificial Intelligence" would be the ability to achieve artificially complex goals. However, this definition does not really bring out the essence of "Artificial Intelligence", so we need to look at this term in more detail first, especially since AI is just having its "Kitty Hawk" moment (On December 17, 1903, the Wright Brothers launched their first powered flight on the beach at Kitt Devil Hills near Kitty Hawk. In commemoration, a drone took off from there on July 17, 2015 for a drug shipment that was euphorically celebrated).

---

[1] See Jerry Kaplan, Artificial Intelligence, translation from the English by Guido Lenz, 1st edition, Frechen, 2017, p. 161.

[2] See Max Tegmark, Leben 3.0, Mensch sein im Zeitalter Künstlicher Intelligenz, Berlin, 2017, p. 080.

[3] See Jerry Kaplan, op. cit. p. 16.

[4] See Manuela Lenzen, Artificial Intelligence, What it can do & what awaits us, 2nd ed., Munich, 2018, p. 21 f.

[5] Max Tegmark, op. cit. p. 080.

The provocative term "Artificial Intelligence" (AI) was cleverly chosen by John McCarthy at Dartmouth College in 1955 to generate as much funding as possible for the so-called Darthmouth Conference.

Maliciously, but certainly not entirely seriously, Gröner and Heinecke put it: "AI is the name of everything that doesn't work yet. As soon as it works, it gets a sensible name: Pattern recognition, face recognition, autonomous driving ...".[6] Wolfgang Wahlster, the former president of the German Research Center for Artificial Intelligence would prefer to call AI "future computer science".[7]

"Synthetic"[8] or "Designed"[9] intelligence might have been more apt, but clearly less titillating. The Belgian AI researcher and linguist Luc Steels even cynically said that "fake intelligence" was more appropriate, since AI systems would not make sense of the results they produced.[10]

All these statements refer to the so-called "weak AI". Before we go further into this form of AI, two categorization patterns will be presented:
Internationally recognised is the subdivision into

- Artificial Narrow Intelligence (ANI)
- Artificial General Intelligence (AGI)
- Artificial Super Intelligence (ASI)

ANI, i.e. the "weak" AI, is currently the only AI available. It is limited to performing tasks clearly specified by human "hands". The immense extent to which the functional field of this AI has already spread today and is still growing rapidly is described in detail in Chap. 3.

AGI is a stage of development in which AI has human-like cognitive abilities and to which we are already approaching with "Deep Learning". It is to be expected that this AI stage will actually be realized in the foreseeable future with quantum computers and further software innovations.

Whether, in contrast, ASI, with which AI proves equal to or even trumps the human brain in all areas such as creativity, wisdom and social skills, will ever be achieved is a matter of heated debate among experts (see Chaps. 7 and 8).

Ralf Otte, professor at the Ulm University of Technology breaks down the three-stage AI into five dimensions:

---

[6] Stefan Gröner/Stephanie Heinecke, Kollege KI, Künstliche Intelligenz verstehen und sinnvoll im Unternehmen einsetzen, Munich, 2019, p. 111.

[7] See Thomas Range, op. cit. p. 18.

[8] Uwe Lämmel/Jürgen Cleve, Künstliche Intelligenz, 4th updated edition, Munich, 2012, p. 11.

[9] Paul Davis, Designed Intelligence, in: John Brockmann, op. cit. p. 60.

[10] See Zukunftsinstitut GmbH (ed.), Künstliche Intelligenz, Wie wir KI als Zukunftstechnologie produktiv nutzen können, Frankfurt, 2019, p. 70.

1. The appropriate intelligence—Adequate response to stimuli in the environment (I1)
2. The learning intelligence—independent acquisition of new knowledge (I2)
3. The creative intelligence—knowledge acquirement beyond formal induction and deduction (I3)
4. The conscious intelligence—conscious understanding of knowledge (I4)
5. The Self-Conscious Intelligence—Conscious Understanding of the Ego-Concept (I5)[11]

I1 and I2 correspond to the ANI, I3 roughly to the AGI and I4 and I5 to the ASI. Otte considers I4 and I5 to be technically unfeasible.[12]

And because there is agreement that we are currently still living in times of "weak AI", the book now concentrates on this AI until Chap. 7.

To this end, first some definitions that reveal different foci of AI:

Steven Finlay defines artificial intelligence simply as "replicating human analytical skills and human decision-making abilities."[13] And McCarthy, the "inventor" of AI describes it as "creating a machine that behaves in a way that would be called intelligent if a human behaved that way."[14] In the late 1980s, Carnegie Mellon University in Pittsburgh saw AI quite poetically as "philosophy translated into computer programs."[15] As Goerz puts it, "Artificial intelligence is the study of computational processes that enable us to perceive, conclude, and act."[16] Uebelhart comments, "AI researches how to detect computers'comprehend intelligent behavior or, more generally, how to use computers to solve problems that require intelligence."[17]And best-selling author K. Zweig defines artlessly, "Artificial intelligence (KI) is software that helps a computer to perform a cognitive activity that humans normally do."[18]

Google Brain co-founder and former head of research at Chinese search engine Baidu Andrew Ng define AI very pragmatically: "AI is the new electricity,"[19] making it clear that AI has long since become ubiquitous.

The inclined reader will not be surprised if, after all the versions here, the author narcissistically also gives his own definition: "AI is a method of formalizing real

---

[11]Ralf Otte, Künstliche Intelligenz für Dummies, 1st ed., Weinheim, 2019, p. 45; see also: Walter Simon, Künstliche Intelligenz, Was man wissen muss, Norderstedt, 2019, p. 42.

[12]Ibid, p. 72.

[13]See Alexander Armbruster, Artificial Intelligence for Everyone, How We Benefit from Smart Computers, 1st ed., Frankfurt a. M., 2018, p. 33.

[14]Ibid, p. 72.

[15]See Klaus Mainzer, KI-Künstliche Intelligenz, Grundlagen intelligenter Systeme, 2003, Darmstadt, p. 25.

[16]Günther Görz/Josef Schneeberger/Ute Schmid, op. cit. p. 1.

[17]Uwe Lämmel/Jürgen Cleve, op. cit., p. 13.

[18]Katharina Zweig, An Algorithm Has No Tact, 3rd ed. Munich, 2019, p. 126.

[19]See Walter Simon, Künstliche Intelligenz, Was man wissen muss, Norderstedt, 2019, p. 11; Stefan Gröner/Stephanie Heinecke, op. cit. p. 12.

phenomena and problems in a binary way and thus generating outputs in the sense of conclusions, results, instructions for action or activities." In this context, the term "binary" is centrally important in order to make us constantly aware that so far even the most sophisticated large-scale computers, which to a certain extent already simulate quantum technology, can only switch "on" and "off".

And what do we do with AI? Well, we have already been "infested" by it for a long time. Pentland writes: "Global Artificial Intelligence (GAI) already exists. Its eyes and ears are the digital services that exist all around us: Credit cards, satellites for use on Earth, cell phones, and, of course, the pecking of billions of people at the Internet."[20] According to Bach, "AI was probably the most prolific technological paradigm of the information age, but despite an impressive streak of initial success, it hasn't lived up to its promise."[21]

In Chap. 3, we will provide evidence that the "AI winter" has been overcome and AI applications are sprouting into the infinite, even if we should always be aware of the limits of today's AI without euphoria. As Donald Knuth aptly puts it, "AI can now do pretty much everything that requires" thinking, " but hardly any of the things that humans and animals do" mindlessly "-that's somehow much harder."[22]

If we summarize the above, we can rest assured that AI will not be able to overpower or enslave us in the foreseeable future, but that it will make our lives easier and offer us new forms of experience in business and society. We can not escape itanymore, but we can make selective use of it in a self-confident way by not following every faddish trend. I don't want everyone watching me eating via mobile and I don't need Alexa to turn on the lights for me, by which I mean nothing against "smart home". Neither her, Siri or any other chatbot ladies will I offer a conversation as long as my dear wife is still willing to talk to me.—On the other hand, I take the liberty of shaking my head at people who still have trees cut down so they can hold their gazettes up in my face, arms outstretched, on the tram instead of consuming them online on a tablet. I'm also fed up with people who still carry their bank transfers (grumbling that no "bank official" receives them with such an important matter) to the bank letterbox instead of doing their banking online and in "real time" with comfort in their own home.

The author's gratitude for the conveniences that we already experience in our daily lives thanks to AI naturally seems ridiculous compared to the immoderately lofty aspirations of some AI experts. For the eminent AI pioneer Marvin Minsky, the goal of AI was "to overpower death." Andreas Wagener listed the central tasks of AI in a less bombastic way:

- Pattern Recognition
- Forecasts and predictions

---

[20] Alex (Sandy) Pentland, Global Artificial Intelligence is Already Here, in: John Brockman, op. cit. p. 343.

[21] Joscha Bach, Every society gets the AI it deserves, in: John Brockman, op. cit. p. 234.

[22] See Nick Bostrum, Superintelligence, Scenarios of a Coming Revolution, 1st ed. 2014, p. 31.

- Presentation of knowledge and information
- Planning and optimization of processes
- Processing of human language (Natural Language Processing
- Autonomous robotic and self-learning systems
- Learning and derived cognitive skills.[23]

Before I get excited about our typical German "data fear" ("Deutschangst") in Chap. 8, I will first give an outline of the history of AI in Chap. 2.

---

[23] Andreas Wagener, op. cit.

"Do You Know How It Was?": The History of AI

2

History is not a club you can leave at will.
John Major

2.1 Human Desire for Creation: The Prehistory of AI

When today technology freaks rave about future paradisiacal times in which omnipotent robots will relieve us of our laborious tasks, then this is the continuation of a dream of mankind that can be observed since time immemorial, only this time it could finally become reality in the foreseeable future.

But before we speculate about the future in Chap. 8, we would like to take a look back at the development so far.

Already in mystical prehistory, Prometheus failed in his attempt to breathe human life into stone figures: the "humans" refused to be moralized by the muses and broke the stone creatures, as Ludwig van Beethoven dramatically and beautifully depicted in his ballet "The Creatures of Prometheus" (op. 43). And Hephaestus, according to legend, created two mechanical golden servants in his underground forge. The Cypriot artist Pygmalion even begat the daughter Paphos with his ivory statue.

Heron, who taught at the Museion in Alexandria, tried his hand at building automata as early as the first century AD. He created a wind-driven organ and the so-called Heronsball, which demonstrates the expansion force of water vapour and the principle of recoil, and is thus the first water-power machine with written record. However, it seemed to be of no practical use. In contrast, his water-powered automatic temple doors were certainly a convincing proof of God to many believers.

© Springer Fachmedien Wiesbaden GmbH, part of Springer Nature 2021
G. Cisek, *The Triumph of Artificial Intelligence*,
https://doi.org/10.1007/978-3-658-34896-0_2

Albertus Magnus is also said to have already constructed a talking bronze head, the 'Brazen Head' complete with a mechanical servant who opened the door and greeted visitors. Unfortunately, his pupil Thomas Aquinas supposedly destroyed it as the devil's work after his death. And in the sixteenth century, Rabbi Judah Löw in Prague is said to have 'created' the giant Golem to protect Jews from frequent pogroms. According to legend, Löw breathed life into the Golem with a special Hebrew chant. The Golem followed the Rabbi's every instruction and protected the people in the Jewish ghetto. But as he grew larger, he literally became megalomaniacal and out of the Rabbi's control. In his distress, Löw changed the word "emet" (= truth), which he had written on the Golem's forehead, into "met", meaning "death", and thus took Golem's life. Of course, Leonardo da Vinci also tried his hand at automata. For the princely family of the Sforzas, he designed the artificial knight whose arms and legs could move by means of drive components. There is a very pleasing reference to the present for this construct: Mark Rosheim, a robotics expert at NASA, proved the amazing functionality of the "artificial knight" after extensive research in his book "Leonardo's Lost Robots" (published by Springer in 2006).[1]

Jacques de Vaucanson not only created the first fully automatic loom, he also took time as an engineer to construct an automatic flute player in 1937 that had 12 songs in its repertoire. His masterpiece, however, was a mechanical duck made of 400 individual parts that could not only quack, flap its wings, drink water, and even digest grains via an artificial intestine, but also excrete them in a lifelike consistency (see Fig. 2.1). But Devlin only notes disparagingly that despite its admirable abilities, this entity is still not a duck, but neither is it a thinking machine.[2]

The "Chess Turk", which the Austro-Hungarian court official Wolfgang von Kempelen presented in 1789, was to bring the "prehistoric AI" to an inglorious end. Hidden in the supposedly autonomous chess-playing device was a little human being who operated the thing with sophisticated magnetism.

Having outlined the historical attempts at "synthetic biology," as Christopher Langton has named it,[3] we now come to the pivotal period in AI history that laid the crucial groundwork for today's AI developments.

As early as around 1300, the Spaniard Raimundus Lullus (Ramon Llull) had the idea of formalising central scientific findings with letters and symbols. In his work 'Ars magna' he made the attempt to logically link concepts on seven rotating discs by means of his 'logical machine' and to draw syllogistic conclusions from them. This concept is reflected in Leibniz's universal language 'lingua universalis', in which, following the pattern of arithmetic and algebra, certain signs were to correspond to things and certain relations between these signs.[4] Even though he tried in vain throughout his life to complete this

---

[1] See FAZ of 03.01.2017.

[2] Keith Kevin, Human Intelligence with Leverage, in: John Brockmann, op. cit. p. 110.

[3] Christopher Langton, What is Artificial Life?, Memento of March 11, 2007 in the Internet Archive.

[4] See, among others, Hans Werner Arndt, Die Entwicklungsstufen von Leibniz' Begriff einer Lingua Universalis, in: vordenker, Sommer-Edition 2011; Klaus Mainzer, op. cit.

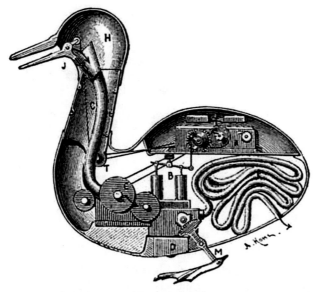

INTERIOR OF VAUCANSON'S AUTOMATIC DUCK.
A, clockwork; *B*, pump; *C*, mill for grinding grain; *F*, intestinal tube;
J, bill; *H*, head; *M*, feet.

Fig. 2.1 Vauconson's duck (Source: Wikimedia Foundation)

'planned language', he did succeed in the 1670s in creating the first calculating machine, which was supposed to perform multiplications and divisions automatically using a staggered roll, but which did not function properly because of the mechanic's lack of manual skill.

For the development of our computers today, however, his attempt at a dual computing machine was an essential step. He writes: "Let a box be provided with holes, that it may be opened and closed. Let it be open at the places corresponding to 1 and closed at the places corresponding to 0. Through the open places let it drop small cubes or balls into small grooves, . . . (see. Fig. 2.2)".[5]

The "hole principle" was then also adopted by Herman Hollerith, but not from Leibnitz, but from Falcon or Josef-Marie Jacquard, who programmed his automatic loom with combinations of holes on paper cards as early as 1728. Before Hollerith, who emigrated from the Pfalz with his parents to the USA, patented his data storage system using punched cards in 1889, Charles Babbage had already been inspired by this punched card system to have the precision mechanic Josef Clement build him a calculating machine, the *difference engine,* in 1832, which was followed by the *analytical engine in* 1833. Almost 50 years

---

[5]Quoted from Torsten Brandes, seminar paper on: The calculating machine of Gottfried Wilhelm Leibnitz, 2003.

Fig. 2.2 Calculating machine
by Leibnitz (Source:
Herrenhausen Palace Museum)

later, Hollerith, together with the physician John Shaw Billings, built the so-called
Hollerith machine for recording cases of illness, in order to record the state of health of
the population with regard to readiness for action in the event of war. The system consisted
of a *tabulating machine*, a punch *card sorter*, a *punch card puncher* and a punch card
reader. It was not until later that 45 of these machines, which Hollerith did not sell but only
rented, were also used for the American and Russian population censuses. In a sense, he
thus developed one of the first operator models, which will be discussed in more detail in
Chap. 6. With 500 employees, the data of the American census were prepared after only
2 years, whereas this had previously taken 7 years.

The author himself was still working with punched cards and punched tape in the 1960s,
but the age of computers had long since begun. As early as 1938, Konrad Zuse had
completed his Z1, the first electrically driven computer with binary numbers, after he had
already built "Zuse's tangerine machine" as a 14-year-old, which gave out fruit and change
when coins were inserted. Whether the latter worked better than the Z1 is not known. In any
case, Zuse was not satisfied with the reliability of the mechanical Z1 and, after he had
already tried out the use of electromechanical relays with the Z2, he constructed the Z3 in
1941 in collaboration with Helmut Schreyer, the first functioning, fully automatic,
program-controlled and freely programmable computer working in binary floating-point
arithmetic and thus the first functioning computer in the world. The Z3 had 600 relays for
the arithmetic unit and 1400 relays for the memory unit. The programs were read in via a
punched tape reader for film strips. The further development as Z4 in 1944 was later used at
the Institute of Applied Mathematics (Institut Angewandte Mathematik) at the ETH Zurich
as the first commercial computer in Europe. There it was also adapted to be "Turing-
compatible".

In 1936, at the same time as Zuse's practical developments, Alan Turing had introduced
the so-called Turing machine,[6] a computer model of theoretical computer science of central
importance for the computer world, which formed the essential basis for the ENIAC
(electronic numerical integrator and computer), which was developed from 1942 onwards
by John Presper Eckert and John William Mauchly at the University of Pennsylvania on

---

[6]See, among others, Thomas Ramge, op. cit. p. 20; Ralf Otte, op. cit. p. 38.

Fig. 2.3 Turing machine (Source: Rocky Astor Turing Machine, reconstructed by Mike Davey as seen at Go Ask ALICE at Harvard University)

behalf of the US Army and presented to the public on February 14, 1946. (The ENIAC could add, subtract, multiply, divide, and take square roots. Incidentally, it was programmed by women, the "ENIAC women": Kay McNulty, Jean Bartik, Betty Holberton, Marlyn Wescoff, Frances Bilas, and Ruth Teitelbaum).

The Turing machine consists of a memory tape with an infinite number of fields on which characters of a predefined alphabet and blanks can be stored. The associated program-controlled read and write head moves back and forth field by field in order to perform calculations with read and input pulses (see Fig. 2.3).

Parallel to Zuse's Z3, the Mark I, also called Automatic Sequence Controlled Calculator (ASCC), was built by IBM in the USA in 1942. It had a weight of 5 (!) tons with a front length of 16 m. This calculator was used by the US Navy between 1944 and 1959 for ballistic calculations, among other things.

Alan Mathison Turing has already been mentioned. But his "Turing machine" was not his only contribution to the development of AI. Rather, the brilliant English mathematician is considered one of the most influential theorists of the early computer age. With the Turing Test he developed, he conceived of a procedure to test whether a machine could have a reasoning ability equivalent to that of a human. He developed this test outline in the essay "Computing Machinery and Intelligence" because he was convinced that intelligence and thought processes could not be formalized and therefore the credibility of the machine with regard to its "human" intelligence could only be proven experimentally. In this test, a human questioner converses via a keyboard and a screen with two interlocutors unknown to him, without having any auditory or visual contact with them. One interlocutor is a human, but the other is a machine. If, after the intensive questioning, the questioner cannot clearly decide which of the two interviewees was the machine, the machine has passed the Turing test, and thus the machine is said to have a reasoning ability equal to that of a human. Turing's assumption that by the year 2000 it would be possible to program computers in such a way that the average user would have at most a 70% chance of successfully identifying a human and a machine after "talking" to them for 5 min was not borne out. In June 2014, a chatbot named Eugene Goostman managed for the first time to convince more than 30% of a jury that it was human. However, the chatbot with the persona of a 13-year-old Ukrainian teenager had no real intelligence, let alone consciousness. The programmer had merely managed to trick the human testers with various strategies. Most chatbots today would certainly pass this test without bluffs. Criticism of this experimental model was that it only tested the functionality of the program, but could not prove intentionality or consciousness itself. John Searle, in particular, has used the "Chinese Room" to argue against the Turing test as an insufficient criterion for proving artificial intelligence. In this "thought experiment", one imagines a closed room in which a person who understands no Chinese at all answers questions posed in Chinese writing—using instructions written in his native language—in a meaningful way. People outside the room infer from the results that the person in the room is proficient in Chinese, even though this is not the case. The experiment was designed to show that a computer can run a program and change strings of characters based on rules without understanding the meaning of the characters.

Nevertheless, it should be noted that the Turing test was not only a repeated occasion to revive the myth of the thinking machine. His work on theoretical computer science will be discussed in Chap. 3.

2.2   The Year of Creation 1956: A New Computer Science Discipline Is Born

So much of the prehistory of AI has been described without the term "artificial intelligence" even being in use up to this point. We owe this term to the Turing Award winner John McCarthy, who used this lurid expression for the first time in his application to the Rockefeller Foundation for funding of a conference in the amount of US$13,500 together with the other applicants Marvin Minsky, Nathaniel Rochester and Claude Shannon from Dartmouth College (founded in 1769 as a school for American Indians, also known as "Big Green") in a promotionally effective manner. The application was approved and so in the summer of 1956 the so-called Dartmouth Conference (official title: Dartmouth Summer Research Project on Artificial Intelligence) took place in Hanover (New Hampshire, USA), which was attended by Ray Solomonoff, Oliver Selfrigde, Trenchard More, Arthur Samuel, Herbert A. Simon and Allen Newell in addition to the applicants. Thus a new computer science discipline was created. According to the application, the conference dealt with the following topics:

1. Automated Computers,
2. How does a computer have to be programmed in order to use language,
3. Neural Networks,
4. Theoretical considerations on the scope of an Arithmetic operation,
5. Self-Improvement,
6. Abstractions,
7. Randomness and creativity.

This conference laid the foundation for ambitious visions in the fields of mathematics, engineering, psychology and many other sciences. Moore's Law by Gordon Moore's (co-founder of Intel) in the 1960s, according to which the complexity of integrated circuits with minimal component costs regularly doubles (annually), naturally spurred the confidence of scientists that the singularity could be achieved in the foreseeable future.

As early as 1957, not long after the Dartmouth Conference, Herbert Simon and Allen Newell introduced their concept of the "General Problem Solver" (GPS). The GPS was based on the principle of problem reduction. In this method, a problem is decomposed into appropriate subproblems in such a way that it can be solved by combining the obtained solutions for the individual subproblems to form a reasonable overall solution. This method is alternatively contrasted with problem transformation, in which a problem is transformed into another problem whose solution is already known or can be found effortlessly. However, it turned out that the GPS could only handle well-defined tasks such as theorems from logic and geometry, word puzzles or chess games.

In 1958, the New York Times reported on a "learning" computer that could tell right from left after 50 trials.[7] Before that, however, in 1952 John von Neumann, one of the important early AI pioneers, had already put into operation the IAS computer he had developed at the Institute for Advanced Study (IAS) in Princeton, which was used primarily for military purposes (e.g. ballistic calculations). Robert Noyce ("Mayor of Silicon Valley"), co-founder of Fairchild Semiconductor and Jack Kilby ("father" of the microchip) of Texas Instruments introduced the first integrated circuits. Kilby's circuit was made of germanicum, Noyce's chip was already made of silicon. In the same year J. McCarthy developed the program language LISP (list processing) on the basis of the Lambda-calculus of Alonzo Church and Stephen Cole Kleene,[8] which was of fundamental importance and is still in use today with the further developments "Common Lisp" and "Scheme". Even the first version could not only process lists, but already knew tree data structures, automatic data storage and recursion, which already constituted a macro system.

Before that, John W. Backus had begun to develop the FORTRAN (FORmula TRANslation) programming language at IBM in 1953. For this programming language, a compiler was constructed under his direction, which reached market maturity in 1957 and was supplied with every IBM 704 system. The European counterpart PROLOG (PROgramming in LOGic), which is "oriented on the structure of the formal language of predicate logic"[9] (see Chap. 3), did not come onto the market until the 1970s. In addition to FORTRAN for programming mainly technical-scientific applications, COBOL (Common Business Oriented Language) was also developed at the end of the 1950s for commercial problems, especially for handling large amounts of data. COBOL was used in particular on

---

[7] See Gernot Brauer, op. cit. p. 16.

[8] See Klaus Mainzer, op. cit. p. 22; Thomas Ramge, op. cit. p. 34.

[9] Klaus Mainzer, op. cit. p. 23.

the UNIVAC I (UNIversal Automatic Computer I), the first commercial computer, which was first delivered by the Remington Rand computer company as early as 1951.

Arthur Samuel did not develop his own computer language, but he did generate an adaptive checkers game on the IBM 701 in 1956, which he continued to work on into the 1970s.

An important AI step was taken in 1959 by Frank Rosenblatt of Cornell University with his publication on the perceptron, a simplified artificial neural network.[10] As early as 1943, Warren Sturgis McCulloch and Walter Pitts had introduced the term "neutron" into computer science as a logical threshold element with multiple inputs and a single output.

In 1964, John G. Kemeny, Thomas E. Kurtz and Mary Kenneth Keller at Dartmouth College developed the education-oriented programming language BASIC (Beginner's All-purpose Symbolic Instruction Code), which was intended to be universally applicable and easy for beginners to learn. Bill Gates will later realize his Microsoft software in BASIC together with his school friend Paul Allen.

Even before the first AI winter,[11] the first mobile robot named Shakey was constructed in 1965 under the direction of Charles Rosen in the artificial intelligence laboratory of the Stanford Research Institute. His development already combined robotics, image processing and natural language processing by recognizing a platform with a block on it after entering the appropriate command and, after also sensing the ramp, pushing it to the platform, rolling over the ramp and then pushing the block off the platform.

In 1966, the ILLIAC (Illinois Automatic Computer) III from the series of mainframe computers built by the University of Illinois between 1951 and 1974 went into operation. It was specially designed for image processing. In the same year, Joseph Weizenbaum of MIT presented his program ELIZA, based on the play Pygmalion by George Bernard Shaw, which simulates the dialogue of a psychotherapist with a patient. All that mattered to Weizenbaum was that the answers and questions appeared "human." This is the so-called "Eliza effect", which is exploited by many chatbots today.

In 1970, as a graduate student of Marvin Minsky at MIT, Terry Allen Winograd developed SHRDLU (derived from ETAOIN SHRDLU, the first two vertical rows of keys on the Linotype typesetting machine), a program that would attempt to converse in natural language over a toy world of toy blocks, demonstrating the difficulties of program-ming natural dialogue.[12]

Chapter 4 will report in detail on applications of AI in medicine. But already in 1972 the expert system MYCIN was developed at Standford University in the already mentioned

---

[10] See Frank Rosenblatt, The perceptron—a probabilistic model for information storage and organi-zation in the brain, in: Psychological Review 65, 1958.

[11] See, inter alia, Manuela Lenzen, op. cit., p. 24; Evegeny Morozov, Smarte Neue Welt, Digitale Technik und die Freiheit des Menschen, 1st ed., Munich, 2013, p. 5.

[12] See Klaus Mainzer, op. cit. p. 23.

program language LISP (list processing), which was used for the diagnosis and therapy of infectious diseases by antibiotics.[13]

Kenneth Colby generated the software program PARRY at Stanford University in 1975, which imitated a person with paranoid schizophrenia and could "talk" to others, sparking serious debate about the possibility and nature of machine intelligence.[14]

In 1975 Bill Gates and Paul Allen founded the software company Microsoft, after the two had already developed the BASIC interpreter Altair BASIC for the new home computer Altair 8800 in 1974.

In 1976, Steve Wozniak, Steve Jobs and Ron Wayne set up Apple's first operating site in Cupertino in a garage to produce personal computers. Prior to this, Frederick Emmons Terman, Dean at Stanford University, had laid out the Stanford Industrial Park near the university from 1952 onwards and persuaded William B. Shockley to set up his semiconductor laboratory there, where semiconductors were manufactured from silicon. In a sense, this was the starting signal for Silicon Valley, in which the orchards of the semi-desert peninsula south of San Francisco very quickly gave way to the computer industry start-ups supported by Terman with venture capital, and Santa Clara Valley developed into the world's most important location for IT companies to date. The fact that the "world spirit" ("Weltgeist") manifested itself there, as Gumbrecht[15] puts it, is certainly due to nearby Stanford University, which transformed itself into an elite university in the 1970s. And if Precht associates this spirit only with "an age of money",[16] he is surely doing an injustice to the multi-billionaires there, for according to the law of diminishing marginal returns (short form: the first beer tastes better to the thirsty than the twentieth!), they are no longer primarily concerned with more billions, but with "making the impossible possible" with the gelt, as the knowledgeable Gumbrecht repeatedly emphasizes.

The AI euphoria of the 1960s was followed by a certain disillusionment in the following decade, because the expected great leaps in quality of AI failed to materialize and the limits of the AI approach first became apparent with Marvin Minsky's and Seymour Papert's book on perceptrons.[17] This period is therefore referred to as the first AI Winter, when research funding, start-up funding and investment in AI plummeted in the "valley of disappointment". A major contributing factor was the 1973 report by James Lighhill, commissioned by the British Parliament, which stated that AI could do no more than

---

[13] See Klaus Mainzer, op. cit. P. 24.

[14] See Manuela Lenzen, op. cit. p. 26.

[15] Hans Ulrich Gumbrecht, Weltgeist im Silicon Valley: Leben und Denken im Zukunftsmodus, Zurich, 2018.

[16] Richard David Precht, Artificial Intelligence and the Meaning of Life, Munich 2020, p. 11.

[17] Marvin Minsky and Seymour Papert, Perceptrons: An Introduction to Computational Geometry, 1st ed., Cambrigde MA 1969.

could be achieved by other sciences and that AI was at best useful for computer games.[18] The first AI winter was followed by others, as will be reported later.

In the late 1990s, AI began to pick up steam again. In 1983, AI visionary Raymond Kurzweil founded the Kurzweil Music System company, demonstrating a new use for AI, an idea that grew out of his friendship with Stevie Wonder. His more substantial contribution to AI, however, is as a non-fiction writer on topics such as health, transhumanism, the technological singularity, and futurology. He predicts an exponential increase in information-technological development by the year 2045: a singularity that will enable an artificial intelligence with which humanity can achieve immortality. In addition to his inspiring theoretical writings, however, he also demonstrated a very beneficial practical approach. As early as 1975 he invented the Kurzweil Reading Machine in close collaboration with blind people.

He stands, in a sense, as a mediator between the building stage of AI and the period in which "weak AI" gradually approaches "strong AI", as will be explained in the next section.

2.3   "Because We Don't Know What They Are Doing": The AI Is Taking on a Life of Its Own

The LSTM (Long Short-Term Memory), which Sepp Hochreiter and Jürgen Schmidhuber introduced in 1997 and later improved by Felix Geers and his team, created a crucial basis for an essential boost in AI performance.[19]

Now impressive application successes were also becoming apparent: the chess computer "Deep Blue" (in reference to IBM's nickname "Big Blue") developed by Fenghsuing Hsu at IBM beat the then world chess champion Kasparov in a game with regular time controls in 1996 and won the whole competition with six games under tournament conditions against him in 1997. Technically, Deep Blue was not yet a learning system.

Only the "AlphaGo" developed by Google DeepMind could claim that. Google Inc. had been founded in 1998 by Larry Page and Sergey Brin in Mountain View and had installed DeepMind as its subcontractor next to the Google search engine. Unlike Deep Blue, AlphaGo no longer works with so-called brute-force algorithms, but with Monte Carlo algorithms, which were used to achieve a breakthrough from 2006 and beat the reigning European champion and professional Go player Fan Hui in 2015. AlphaGo was already using machine learning techniques. Google launched the further development in 2017 as AlphaZero, which also achieved a 3–0 victory against the best Go player in the world, Ke

---

[18] See, among others, Günther Görz/Josef Schneeberger/Ute Schmid, op. cit. p. 5; Thomas Ramge, op. cit. p. 36; Walter Simon, Artificial Intelligence, What You Need to Know, Berlin, 2019, p. 34; The Dark Ages of AI: A Panel Discussion at AAAI-84, in: AI Magazine. Volume 6 Number 3 (1985).

[19] See Axel Armbruster, op. cit. p. 17.

Jie. The main difference to its predecessor is that it taught itself the game with so-called "unsupervised learning" (see Chap. 3, Sect. 3.3) in only 24 h, and not only the game of Go, but also chess and shogi at the same time.

But IBM had not stopped at Deep Blue either. In the meantime, they had developed the Watson computer program (after Thomas J. Watson, one of IBM's first presidents) to provide answers to questions entered in digital form in natural language. To demonstrate its capabilities, the program successfully competed with two human opponents who had previously won record sums on the show in three episodes of the quiz show "Jeopardy!" that aired from February 14–16, 2011. Watson's software engine is DeepQA. DeepQA was written in various programming languages; including Java, C++ and Prolog. DeepQA is implemented here in the form of annotators (annotators are software tools that make annotations, correction notes, etc.) of a UIMA (Unstructured Information Management Architecture) pipeline. By using UIMA Asynchronous Scaleout and Hadoop, massive parallelization is made possible.

In the mid-2000s, a new phenomenon emerged that is directly related to AI: social media.

LinkedIn was founded in 2003 by Reid Hoffman and founding members of PayPal and Socialnet.com (Allen Blue, Eric Ly, Jean-Luc Vaillant, Lee Hower, Konstantin Guericke, Stephen Beitzel, David Eves, Ian McNish, Yan Pujante and Chris Saccher) with headquarters in Mountain View, California. Since February 4, 2009, the network is also available in German. LinkedIn is a web-based social network for maintaining existing business contacts and making new business connections.

Facebook is founded in 2004 by Mark Elliot Zuckerberg along with his flat share partners and Harvard College students Eduardo Saverin, Andrew McCollum, Dustin Moskovitz and Chris Hughes in Cambridge, MA and could be used on PCs as well as tablets and smartphones. Previously, in 2003, Mark Zuckerberg created the website facemash.com, the predecessor of Facebook, while studying psychology and computer science at Harvard University. It was a rating system for women's looks that was only public for a few days due to protests (I remember us pubescent high school students using an AI and gender distant scale of 1–10 for this, which conversely was probably in use by our female classmates). Zuckerberg posted photos of female students on the Internet without their permission and asked visitors to the site to choose the more attractive of two randomly selected photos.

Twitter is a microblogging service of the company Twitter Inc., which was founded in 2006 in San Francisco by Jack Dorsey, Biz Stone and Evan Williams. On Twitter, logged-in users can distribute telegram-like short messages. The messages are called "tweets".

Instagram is part of Facebook and was created in 2010 by Kevin Systrom and Mike Krieger. It is an ad-supported online service for sharing photos and videos. Instagram is a mixture of microblog and audiovisual platform and allows photos to be shared on other social networks.

Why these two web services could be benevolently given the designation "**social media**" will probably remain hidden from the author (see Chap. 7), but their increasing social influence cannot be denied in any case.

In 2000, the term "Deep Learning" finally appeared for the first time, which Jürgen Schmidhuber claims is just a new term for artificial neural networks. After all, it is fair to say that Deep Learning is currently the most advanced and promising type of machine learning and will therefore occupy a central place in the following chapter on AI techniques.

How Does AI Function?: AI Techniques

3

Technology may not save us time, but it distributes it differently.
Helmar Nahr

In many books on AI, this chapter begins with the author's considerate advice to skip it if you lack an affinity for formal logic.

With the promise to present the facts as comprehensible as possible, I strongly recommend to "bite through" the chapter in order to get an idea of the complexity behind the abbreviation AI.

3.1 The World in "On"/"Off" Mode: Formal Logic

AI is computer-technically limited to grasping and "processing" the real world with only two states, namely, "on" or "off" or binary with "0" or "1". Quite some scientists doubt, this is possible at all. For example, the publicist Morozov asks critically: "But is truth a binary function? It may be—if one arrogantly assumes that one's values and interests are the only" right "values and interests. Technocratic thinking regards pluralism as an enemy, not an ally—or in geek parlance: a bug, not a feature."[1] And Ralf Otte has a personal answer to this question: no, nature is not "mechanizable."[2] In doing so, he refers to the fundamental critique of the physicist Penrose, who believes that artificial intelligence is not

---

[1] Evegeny Morozov, op. cit. p. 233.
[2] Ralf Otte, op. cit., p. 283.

worth its name because, unlike human intelligence, it is only algorithmic.[3] In fact, algorithms are still the tool of computer-adequate formalization today, as will be shown in the next section. Yet there were very early attempts to develop formal or symbolic languages. In the "Organon", the compilation of his most important writings on the philosophy of language, logic and the philosophy of science, Aristotle already shows a formal language for propositional logic in the fourth century BC, as it is still used today. In his work "Ars magna", the Mallorcan philosopher Ramon Llull (lat.: Raimundus Lullus), as already mentioned in more detail in Chap. 1, tries to formalize truths of different fields of knowledge with a combination of letters and symbols already at the end of the fourteenth century. Leibnitz's "lingua universalis" is also already a symbolic language, which assigns certain signs to things and allot certain relations between these signs. Since the 1960s, cognitive science has been endeavouring to realise cognitive abilities in machines on the basis of the assumption that the brain is an information-processing system and works in principle like a computer—undoubtedly an enormous challenge.

If one considers that the decimal number 10 in binary system is represented as "1010", but already the decimal number 100 in binary is represented as "1,100,100" and the romantic sentence "I love you" soberly transforms into "01001001 01100011 01101000 00100000 01101100 01101001 01100101 01100010 01100101 00100000 01100100 01101001 01100011 01101000" according to ASCII code, one can imagine the infinite sequences of numbers that result even in the operationalization of trivial problems. On the other hand, however, Nvidia's Xavier chip already managed 30–35 trillion arithmetic operations per second.[4] The Sunway TaihuLight in Wuxi is already pushing 125 petaflops (125,000,000,000,000 calculations/sec) in 2019. And by the time this book is published, there will certainly be several more flops (floating point operations per second).

To formalize or digitize our multifaceted universe in a computer-friendly way requires sophisticated logic and complex techniques, which can only be outlined in this book to the extent that those concerned with AI can at least guess at the challenges facing the "AI makers". Let's start with the foundation of all digitization: algorithms.

3.1.1   Algorithms

The term "algorithm"probably does not derive from the Greek "álgiros" (painful), but probably goes back to the Arab scholar Abu Dscha'far Muhammad ibn Musa al-Chwārizmī (Latinized Algorismi), who wrote a mathematical textbook in the ninth century.

The definition of this exotic term is disappointingly simple: "Algorithms are—to put it vividly—solution-oriented processing rules that are intended to solve a specific task or

---

[3] See ibid.

[4] Alexander Armbruster, op. cit. p. 68.

problem".[5] Or, as Volland puts it in a pleasing way: "An algorithm is also nothing technical in the first place. It is the term used to describe any unambiguous instruction for solving problems—even cooking recipes or traffic rules are simple algorithms."[6]

Of course, "simple algorithms" do not solve most of the problems faced by AI. But the fact remains: no matter how complex the task, the algorithm(s) used only develop binary sequences of 0 and 1 during implementation.

This also applies to so-called "genetic algorithms", which approach the optimal problem solution step by step according to the evolution principle in a simulation process. Mike Müller and Dennis Freese write: "Genetic algorithms are heuristic optimization methods. This means that normally too much effort is needed for optimal solutions and therefore assumptions (heuristics) are made to help find a solution. Normally, only parameters of an equation, formula or in another given form of a structured solution approach are optimized. That's why they are applied where the problem is not well understood or their solution is not solvable due to computational and mathematical reasons."[7] This is especially true for Deep Learning, which is discussed in more detail in Sect. 3.2.4.

If all this sounds too theoretical for you, let me quote the publicist Gernot Brauer: "So what are algorithms really? As I said, they are programs that solve mathematical tasks. However, they can be linked—as is often done—with actuators, i.e. with devices that transmit digital decisions to the physical world and trigger action depending on algorithm signals, for example in the automotive industry when steering, accelerating or braking cars without a human driver depending on what sensors calculate about their environment."[8] Or to put it more succinctly, an algorithm is an instruction for action to produce useful output data by processing input data.[9]

Donald Ervin "Don" Knuth, the leading expert on algorithms, distinguishes between "fundamental", "seminumerical", "combinatorial" and "syntactic" algorithms. Fundamental algorithms are basic programming problems such as greedy algorithms that use heuristics to generate fast, not always optimal solutions, or graph algorithms that solve the "queueing theorem" or the "traveling salesman problem." Seminumerical algorithms are a mixture of numerical and analytical or algebraic methods, used for example in computer algebra systems (e.g. to illustrate graphically functions and data in two or three dimensions). Combinatorial algorithms are complex formulas for representing three-dimensional structures, and syntactic algorithms are used in neuro-linguistic programming or speech recognition.

---

[5] Andreas Syska/Philippe Lievre, Illusion 4.0, Germany's naive dream of the smart factory, 2016, p. 66.

[6] Holger Volland, Die kreative Macht der Maschinen, Warum Künstliche Intelligenzen bestimmen, was wir morgen fühlen und denken, 1st ed.

[7] Mike Müller/Dennis Freese, Genetic Algorithms in: Project for Algorithmic Applications, Cologne, p. 4.

[8] Gernot Brauer, op. cit. p. 85.

[9] Cf. Ralf Otte, op. cit. p. 279.

For the classification of algorithm ontologies, Katharina Zweig introduces the ethical aspect and groups all algorithmic decision-making systems under the term "algoscope" "that make decisions about people, resources that affect people, and those decisions that change the social participation opportunities of people."[10]

Let's close the section with Pedro Domingos' vision of a learning "master algorithm",[11] the invention of which would enable humanity to sit back and relax, because the learning machine equipped in this way would take over all tasks independently.—However, this would require a powerful AI, which is not yet in sight. Therefore, in the next sections, we will again turn modestly to other AI techniques.

3.1.2   Propositional Logic/Causality

In the last section, we learned that algorithms form the basis of AI. Logical procedures lend themselves to the modeling of their instruction sequences. Before we turn to the most important of these, we will first introduce, in rudimentary form, some central symbols and basic concepts that are used in standard logics such as propositional and predicate logic:

- Logical values: true = 1; false = 0
- Conjunction = A **and** B (formula sign: $\wedge$ = conjunct) $\Rightarrow$ A $\wedge$ B
- Disjunction = A **or** B (formula symbol: v = disjunctor) $\Rightarrow$ A v B
- Exclusion = not A or **not** B (formula symbol: $\neg$ = negator) $\Rightarrow$ $\neg$ A or $\neg$ B
- Implication = **if** A **then** B (formula symbol: $\rightarrow$ = implicator)
- Equivalence = A **is equal to** B (formula sign: $\leftrightarrow$ = tautology)[12]

These terms are explained below:

A conjunction is a statement composed of two statements which claims that both partial statements are true.

Example: Statement A: 4 is divisible by 2; Statement B: 4 is a square number. Both are true, so A $\wedge$ B is true (spoken: A and B).

A non-exclusive disjunction (also called an adjunction) is a compound statement that asserts that at least one of its partial statements is true. Disjunction in this sense is also

---

[10] Katharina Zweig, op. cit. p. 25.

[11] Pedro Domingos, The Master Algorithm: How the Quest for the Ultimate Learning Machine Will Remake Our World, New York, 2015.

[12] See inter alia Gerd Harbeck, Einführung in die formale Logik, 2nd Amended Edition, Braunschweig, 1966, p. 15 ff; Andreas Dengel/Ansgar Bemardi/Ludger van Elst, Wissenspräsentation in: Andreas Dengel, (ed.), Semantic Technologies, Foundations - Concepts - Applications, Heidelberg, 2012, p. 25 ff; Fabrizio Riguzzi, Foundations of probabilistic logic programming, Languages, Semantics, Inference and Learning, Gistrup, 2018, p. 4 ff; Ralf Otte, op. cit. p. 121 ff; Günther Görz/Josef Schneeberger/Ute Schmid, op. cit. p. 142.

called *non-exclusive or*. That "at least" one sub-statement is true naturally includes that all sub-statements can be true. So the statement is false only if A and B are false. The exclusionary disjunction (also called contravalence) states that only one of the two statements involved is true (either ... or). The exclusionary disjunction is therefore false if either both statements involved are false or if both statements involved are true.

To make the difference clear, the two truth tables are shown below.

Non-exclusive disjunction:

A	B	A ∨ B
True	True	True
True	wrong	True
wrong	True	True
wrong	wrong	wrong

A:4 is divisible by 2	B: 4 is a square number
A:4 is divisible by 2	B: 4 is not a square number
A: 4 is not divisible by 2	B: 4 is a square number
A: 4 is not divisible by 2	B: 4 is not a square number

Excluding disjunction

A	B	A ∨ B
True	True	wrong
True	wrong	True
wrong	True	True
wrong	wrong	wrong

A:4 is divisible by 2	B: 4 is a square number
A:4 is divisible by 2	B: 4 is not a square number
A: 4 is not divisible by 2	B: 4 is a square number
A: 4 is not divisible by 2	B: 4 is not a square number

The exclusion (also called Sheffer's stroke "↑" or NAND = "not and") is the negation of the conjunction. The total statement of two statements linked by the Sheffer's stroke is true if at least one statement is false, or false if both are true. This results in the truth table below:

A	B	A ↑ B
True	True	wrong
True	wrong	True
wrong	True	True
wrong	wrong	True

The material implication, also called conditional or subjunction, expresses the sufficient condition: It says that the truth of one sub-statement is a sufficient condition for the truth of the other sub-statement.

The term "equivalence" is certainly self-explanatory. But the logical expressions just theoretically presented will hopefully become a little more understandable with the explanations below.

In propositional logic, each statement is assigned a truth value, namely 1 for "true" and 0 for "false" (bivalence principle) and the traditional epistemological principle applies: "tertium non datur" (English: Law of the Excluded Middle, LEM), i.e.: a third is not given. So it follows A (=statement) v ¬ B (either A or not A). In the concrete example: "Eve is pregnant (A) or not pregnant (B)"—there is no such thing as "a little pregnant". In this context, perhaps one or the other reader still remembers the Fulda Bishop Dyba, who repeatedly railed: "A bit of Catholic is not possible." But this still does not clarify whether statement A ("Eve is pregnant") receives the truth value 1. But if Eve is indeed pregnant, then the disjunction becomes invalid and ¬ B holds.

The simplest statements, which cannot be further decomposed within the framework of propositional logic, are also called atomic. This logic examines statements that are characterized by the fact that the truth value of a statement composed of simpler components depends only on the truth value of the partial statements and not on their content. And this can be quite confusing at times. For example, the statement "When horses fly, ice is cold." is true because the succedent is true, even though the antecedent (When horses fly) is big nonsense. Similarly, the statement "When horses fly, ice melts" is true because both the antecedent and the succedent are false.

With *the modus ponens* better *modus ponendo ponens* another statement can be inferred from two true statements. Example: All humans are mortal. Günter Cisek is a human being. Consequently, Günter Cisek is mortal. Or generally speaking: If statement a implies statement b and a is true, then b is also true.

This should suffice to explain propositional logic. Let us now turn to the directly related "causal logic":

To clarify a common misunderstanding right away—correlations are not causalities, as will be explained in the section "Big Data". Causality is not "**if** . . ., then", but "**because** . . ., then", i.e. the correlation can be assigned to a cause. Thus, an event A is the cause of event B (B < A). A counterfactual implication also involves a causal relation: "If Robert were not my son, Mimi would not be my granddaughter." Thus, causation exists only if event B (Mimi) would not have occurred if event A (Robert) had not occurred.

Now, if the curious reader wants to know more about Mimi and Robert, an appropriate technique for doing so would be predicate logic, which will be characterized in the next section.

3.1.3   Predicate Logic

Predicate logic (also quantifier logic) is a special form of knowledge representation that is frequently used in the programming languages LISP and Prolog, among others.[13] Compared to propositional logic, it opens up more extensive symbol structures and plays an important role in the conception and programming of expert systems.[14] Predicate logic was essentially developed by the linguistic philosopher Friedrich Ludwig Gottlob Frege and Charles Sanders Peirce from the USA.

Predicate logic assigns properties (predicates) to objects and uses "quantifiers". Quantifiers indicate by how many individuals of the discourse universe a propositional function is fulfilled. The most common are

- The **existential quantifier** or **particulate** $\exists$ i.e., "at least one element (x) has property F" ($\exists x F x$).
- the **all-quantor** or **universal quantifier** $\forall$ i.e.: "all/every element of the basic set ($x_{1,2}$ ... x_n has property F" ($\forall x F x$).

If one wanted to formalize the statement "a red cherry" in predicate logic, one would first have to formulate: "There is at least one cherry (M as a property of x) and it is red (R as a property of x)."

Symbolically, we get $\exists (M(x) \wedge R(x))$.

In contrast, the sentence "All cherries are red" should be rephrased as: "If it's a cherry, it's red".

The formalization is: $\prod x \, (M^*(x) \rightarrow R^*(x))$.
"No cherry is red" would formalize to:

$\neg \exists \, (M(x) \wedge R(x))$.[15]

*M and R are predicates and relation symbols, respectively.
These are examples of first level predicate logic. Multi-level predicate logic is used to form classes, graphs, schemas, or frames.
First, here is an example of formalizing a class (animals) with subclasses:

---

[13] See, among others, Peter Gentsch, Artificial Intelligence for Sales, Marketing and Service, Wiesbaden, 2018, p. 33; Thomas Range, op. cit. p. 34; Uwe Lämmel/Jürgen Cleve, op. cit. p. 69.

[14] Klaus Mainzer, op. cit., p. 42.

[15] See Andreas Dengel, op. cit., p. 31 ff.; Wolfgang Ertel, Grundkurs Künstliche Intelligenz, Eine praxisorientierte Einführung, 4th ed.

	Animals	Vertebrates	Mammals	Fish	Birds
Whale	X	X	X		
Tiger	X	X	X		
Chicken	X	X			X
Carp	X	X		X	
Siskin	X	X			X
Snail	X				

Graphs draw the relations between objects, as known from mindmapping, for example.

The term "schema" was coined by Frederic Charles Bartlett in cognitive psychology. After his experiences with the game "Silent Post", he investigated the way in which existing prior knowledge affected the perception and storage of new information. The results of his investigations led him to the conviction that memory is a kind of collection of schemata which influence perception and thus also memory. A schema is therefore a mental knowledge structure that contains information about a certain object or concept in an abstract, generalized form. If, for example, the schema "hunter" is activated in the counterpart by the perceived person wearing a chamois beard hat, the behavior of the person is then interpreted accordingly on the basis of the information contained in the schema "hunter" in the "perceiver". This effect is called "assimilation".

A visit to a restaurant is often cited as an example of such a memorized pattern: The memorized process follows the schema: read the menu, place the order, eat the food, ask for the bill. Such a restaurant schema controls the expectations of the person, directs his perception and controls his actions and interactions.[16]

The terms "frames" and "scripts" have similar meanings. Roger C. Schank and Robert P. Abelson introduced the term "frame" for objects and their properties and the term "script" for actions. A script, then, is a structure that describes appropriate sequences of events in specific contexts. As an example of such a script, the literature gives the production of cinnamon biscuits.[17] Here, a simpler frame is shown in Table 3.1:

In summary, predicate logic is an extension of propositional logic. It can be used to describe properties of individual objects and their relations to each other on one or more levels. It is thus a valuable tool for the representation of knowledge.

---

[16] See Andreas Dengel, op. cit. p. 56.

[17] See Andreas Dengel, op. cit., p. 41 ff; Manuela Lenzen, op. cit., p. 46.

Table 3.1 Frame for a parasaurolophus

Object	Features	Value
Parasaurolophus	is a	Duckbill Dinosaur
	Weight	2.5 tons
	has	Cranial bone pin
	Length	9,5 m
	Habitat	Pangaea

Table 3.2 Fuzzy logic—value levels

Criterion	Value levels			
Driving speed	Slow	Normal	Quick	Lawn
Numerical conversion	0–30 h/km	80–120 h/km	130–160 h/km	Over 160 h/km
Music tempo (classical)	Largo	Adagio	Andante	Presto
Numerical conversion	42–70[a]	98–124	124–152	180–208
Music tempo (beat)	Slow	Normal	Quick	Exstatic
Numerical conversion	40–60 bpm[b]	60–80 bpm	80–140 bpm	Over 140 bpm

[a]Beats per minute
[b]Beat per minute

However, it proves useless for fuzzy variables that cannot be represented in binary, such as "The weather is quite nice." For this problem, "fuzzy logic"is used, as presented in the next section.

3.1.4   Fuzzy Logic

Many decisions in real life have to be made under uncertainty, and we humans manage this every day. The computer, however, refuses to accept such imprecision. Therefore, fuzzy logic or fuzzinesslogic in pattern recognition was developed to precisely capture the imprecise. It is used to model so-called "hedge expressions" such as fairly, strongly, violently, weakly, or very mathematically precise.

This is done by dividing such a "fuzzy" term as "fairly fast" into precise value levels and thus making it calculable.

Table 3.2 illustrates this process.

But precision also has its reasonable limits. The fact that precision beyond a certain level is not reasonable was pointed out by the founder of fuzzy logic, the mathematician Lotfi A. Zadeh of the University of California Berkeley in 1973 in his "Principle of Incompatibility": "To the same extent that the complexity of a system increases, our ability to make precise and at the same time significant statements about its behavior decreases. Beyond a

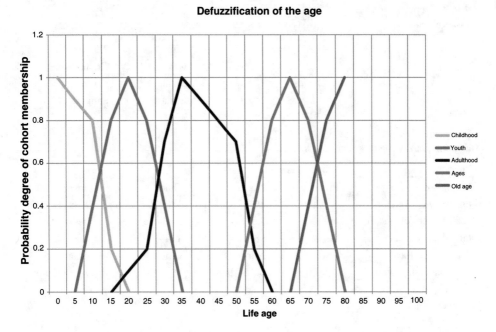

Fig. 3.1 Defuzzification of the age of life

certain threshold, precision and significance (relevance) become almost mutually exclusive properties."[18]

Another approach is the membership function, which has the degree of membership of the element to the definition set, where the value must be between 0 and 1. Here, the degree 1 indicates full membership and 0 indicates no membership at all. Thus, in the example below, an infant has a degree of membership of 1 for the "childhood" age category (see Fig. 3.1) and the author has a degree of 0.8 for the "old age" cohort. The calculation of such an exact value from the fuzzy set is called "defuzzification". With fuzzy logic, therefore, the "vagueness" of linguistic expressions is countered by "fuzzifying" the truth value by the degree of affiliation, i.e. making it programmable.

These fuzzy sets have a very practical meaning. They can be used to program fuzzy rules for so-called "intelligent tools", which we will discuss in more detail in the chapter "Industry 4.0". These rules typically consist of an antecedent, which specifies a fuzzy situation by means of tolerance values, and a consequent, which concludes an instruction from it. A concrete example: The flexibility of a steel sheet changes with its storage time before processing. The pressure of the pressing tool is therefore programmed in a differentiated manner for the different storage times (here = fuzzy quantities).

---

[18]Lotfi A. Zadeh, "Principle of Incompatibility", 1973; Quoted from Hans Jürgen Zimmermann, Prinzipien der Fuzzy Logic, in: Spectrum.de from March 1, 1993.

Another practical use of fuzzy logic is the use of probability statements, which can save considerable capacity in programming. The professionals may forgive the following layman's sketch of the approach: For example, there are about 6900 species of birds and all these birds can fly except for penguins, ostriches and a few other ratites. So the probability that a bird can fly is over 99%. Now instead of programming every time: Bird can fly if not penguin, pretend there are no penguins and assign a truth value of 1. For the vast majority of operations, this will not present a problem. Only if there is rarely a non-plausible result, the error is then detected step by step with the so-called "backpropagation"(= error backpropagation), which will be discussed in more detail in the sections on supervised machine learning.

Nowadays, fuzzy logic plays an important role in control engineering, where it is used in particular in medical, entertainment and automotive engineering. It is a form of so-called 'soft computing' in distinction to the exact numerical methods. The term was introduced by Lotfi A. Zadeh, the founder of fuzzy logic.

This is a fragmentary description of the most important logics used in AI. They form the programmatic foundations for machine learning, to which the next sections are devoted.

3.2   The Human Steers, the Machine Thinks—Machine Learning

Machine learning (ML) has become the central technique of AI. ML stands for the "artificial" or machine generation of knowledge based on large amounts of data. What is essential here is that the result-oriented algorithms are no longer programmed by humans; instead, the tasks are performed by machine learning from the input data, in which the system recognizes patterns and regularities and analyzes the data accordingly and makes decisions as necessary. These ML algorithms are constructed in such a way that they constantly improve themselves in a "learning" manner when they are provided with further data, thus making model adaptations possible.

This is where AI comes to the point where it has an advantage over human intelligence. While the human brain finds it difficult to recognize meaningful patterns for more than 7–8 variables in a comprehensive data set, the computer manages this effortlessly for hundreds of variables in a short time. In this context, one also speaks of the "automation of intelligent behavior".[19]

There are different types of learning and divergent content focus of the learning systems, which will be explained in more detail in the next sections.

---

[19] Katharina Zweig, op. cit. p. 125.

3.2.1   Supervised Learning

The term "supervised learning"already indicates that here the user still remains in control of the situation, since he is largely in charge of the analysis process. The term "learning" is actually a bit too homoaffine and should better be replaced by "training" or "cramming", because the computer does not yet succeed in "grasping" learning, as a student does, for example.

The essence of supervised learning is that training is done with input and output data that are known and thus the learning outcome is measurable. A solution already exists for the problem and the AI learns from these examples. The comparison between predicted and actual output value is allowed during training in order to gradually improve the model and thus make better predictions.

The prerequisite for the training process is that the program developer segments a training set and a test set from the large mass of data on which the computer can define and solve the knowledge problem. The data set is determined by the complexity of the "true function". For example, if there is multiple interdependence between the input variables, a much larger amount of data is required than for a one-dimensional relationship. The "supervisor" (expert) first assembles the "correct" training set. The training data must be set in such a way that they correspond to the so-called "hypothesis" or the two selected parameters. Thus, if the learning algorithm is to arrive at distinguishing cats from dogs, cat and dog images must also be provided. When the training algorithm has detected patterns, these found models are processed to results (output) by the inferential or predictive algorithm. Now comes the quality control stage, in which the test data is analyzed using the processed model. For the test data set the correct results ("ground truth"/"labels") are available without the computer knowing them. The deviation of the computer results from the actual data indicates the degree of accuracy of the model. By adding new or different parameters to the analysis model that the computer has created based on the input data, this quality measure can be improved. However, this optimization process has its limitations. If the specification of the model contains too many explanatory variables, so-called "overfitting"occurs, so that the coefficient of determination of the prediction or the correlation factor decreases. Here the "Occam's razor" can help, which tries to arrive at the result with the simplest theory or with the simplest decision tree. However, this can also lead to "underfitting".

This makes it clear how important it is to predefine "reasonable features" (characteristics) already in the training set, which are derived from experience or expert knowledge and generate good predictor variables. According to Pedro Domingos, this feature engineering is the most exciting act in the learning process.[20] Care must also be

---

[20] See Pedro Domingos, A few useful things to know about machine learning in: Communications of the ACM. 55 (10), pp. 78–87.

taken to weed out so-called "noise" in the training set, i.e. to filter out inappropriate data sets such as irrelevant, incorrect or extreme values.

In supervised learning, we distinguish between two learning problems or outcome goals: regression and classification. In regression, the model detects correlations between different variables (e.g., typical sales of goods on certain calendar days). It should be emphasized here that this learning process—and this applies to all types of machine learning—only detects correlations, but not causalities (!).

This represents a decisive paradigm shift in research. The author, still influenced by the empirical social research of the Cologne School, would have been tempted to first create a deductively derived hypothesis for the training set in order to verify its "correctness" on the data run or to falsify it with the null hypothesis. The term is deliberately placed in quotation marks because empirical statements can never be verified, at most falsified. If explanatory causalities no longer play a role, it is advisable, at least in the case of surprising correlations, even if they are statistically significant, to check the training set to see whether any third-party variables could be a cause.

Models for regression are the regression line and the regression tree. The regression line shows the correlation between the independent variable and the target variable and results from the minimum square distance of the data points from the trend line. The strength of the relationship is measured by the correlation coefficient between 0 and 1. The regression tree is a binary decision tree in which each "leaf" (= graph end) predicts a numerical quantity.

In classification, the data sets are mostly broken down by qualitative features, such as spam mails/non-spam mails with the Naive Bayes filter, where the characteristic words of the mail in question are used to infer properties that are undesirable in the recipient. This example would be "only" a binary classification problem. But also multiple classes can be sorted with supervised learning using decision trees or the support vector method. Such a decision tree starts with a "root node" (e.g. car), from which so-called "edges" lead to "nodes" (e.g. new or old), at which a property of the object is queried. The "answer" of the node decides about the following node (e.g. roadworthy resp. not roadworthy). This procedure continues until one reaches a leaf at which the decision is made (e.g. sellable or not sellable). The "Support Vector Machine" (SVM), which is actually not a machine but a software program, divides a set of objects into classes in such a way that the widest possible area around the class boundaries remains free of objects; it is a so-called large margin classifier. For example, fruit and vegetable varieties are sorted into different quality levels.

Another method for pattern recognition in supervised learning is the K-Nearest Neighbor (KNN) algorithm. In the k-nearest neighbor principle, class assignment is performed considering its k-nearest neighbors. The learning is done by simply storing the training examples, which is also called lazy learning. The method is mainly used for credit evaluation, election prediction and handwriting, image and video recognition.

How well the learning algorithm succeeds in classification can be measured with the Bayes classifier. This classifier, which assigns each object to the class to which it belongs with the greatest probability, is calculated for the test set and then compared with the result of the training set. The deviations between the two sets are minimized by backpropagation of the errors.

The fact that pattern recognition doesn't always work out was shown in a very embarrassing way in 2015 with Google's new photo service. The weighting of the sorting algorithms had led to the black programmer Jack Alciné and his girlfriend, who was also black, being sorted as "gorillas" in a photo album.

Finally, the "bias-variance dilemma" should be pointed out. In modeling the learning algorithm, one must face the incompatibility of simplicity and result accuracy. The "variance" refers to the degree of deviation in the learning outcome between different training sets. If there is a large variance, it is likely that either the homogeneity of the data is not sufficient to produce useful learning results, or the model features of the input space need to be extended. This is contrasted with "bias", which indicates the error that results from simplifying the model. When there is linear functionality between the model variables, simplifying the "hypothesis" is useful, but when the complexity of the real-world problem is high, simplification does not produce useful results.

Another variant of "machine learning" is "unsupervised learning", which we will deal with in the next section.

3.2.2 Unsupervised Learning

In contrast to supervised learning, unsupervised learning knows no supervisor and no known in advance target values.

Rather, the learning machine tries to recognize patterns in the input data itself. Thus, there is no training and testing set. The input space is not pre-sorted, which greatly simplifies data provision.

So in unsupervised learning, the system doesn't know what to recognize. It identifies patterns and divides the data into clusters or categories, but without knowing which categories they are or which label they fall under. The algorithm correctly segments cats from dogs, for example, without training, but without naming them as such.

This already addresses the most common problem in unsupervised learning, namely the so-called cluster analysis. Here, the goal is to arrange a set of data points into a certain number of groups (so-called clusters). Instead of responding to feedback, cluster analysis autonomously identifies commonalities in the data and responds based on the presence or absence of such commonalities in each new piece of data. This approach also helps identify anomalous data points that do not fit into either group.

Learning " here classically takes place according to Hebb's rule. As early as 1949, the psychologist Donald Olding Hebb proved that neurons have common synapses and that the following rule applies: The more often neuron A is active simultaneously with neuron B, the more preferentially the two neurons will react to each other ("what fires together, wires together").

In addition to cluster analysis, unsupervised learning also solves the compression of data for dimensionality reduction. Here, an attempt is made to represent many input values in a more compact form, while losing as little information as possible. For example, Principal Component Analysis can be understood as a compression technique when the least important components of the data are omitted. This is practically equivalent to a linear autoencoder. This is a multilayer artificial neural network whose target values are the input values, with a hidden layer with fewer nodes than input values serving as a "bottleneck". The activations of these neurons are the compressed data, from which the original data should then be reconstructed (decompressed) as well as possible.

The appealing thing about unsupervised learning is that the search algorithm can produce surprising results. With large amounts of data, the computer is clearly superior to the human intellect in terms of pattern recognition. It recognizes correlations that remain hidden even to experts in their field. A well-known example of this is a startling example from cancer research. There, unsupervised data runs have proven that for the prediction of the disease course not only the diseased cells have to be observed, but that the healthy cells in the vicinity of the carcinoma are co-determinants.

Unsupervised learning is the general "understanding" of the data at hand. What is referred to as "knowledge discovery" is ultimately the discovery of hidden structures or relationships in the data. There is, of course, a risk that the individual, once categorized in a cluster, will fall into "algorithmic clannishness".[21]

It is also problematic that the solution path in unsupervised learning—as the name already makes clear—is not comprehensible, but the search process remains a 'black box'. Or as the British-Hungarian philosopher Michael Polanyi put it in the so-called Polanyi Paradox: "We know more than we can tell."[22]

A special form of unsupervised learning is competitive learning "in which individual neurons specialize on subsets of the training data". Competition during training can be either "hard", in which only one neuron is activated for each stimulus and changes its weights (winner-takes-all), or "soft", so that the weights of several neurons are adjusted at each learning step (soft competition).[23] The Mexican-hat function often used here, whose graph has similarities to the profile of a Mexican hat (see Fig. 3.2), is the curve "that reflects the degree to which the change in weights is affected."[24]

For the sake of completeness, "semisupervised learning" should be mentioned here. As the term suggests, this is a cross between supervised and unsupervised learning.

In semi-supervised learning, a small amount of labeled data is provided with a large amount of unlabeled data in the input space. This is because it has been noticed that unlabeled data, when used with a small amount of labeled data, can provide a significant

---

[21] Katharina Zweig, op. cit. p. 229.

[22] See Thomas Ramge, op. cit. p. 17.

[23] See Thomas Ramge, op. cit. p. 251.

[24] Thomas Ramge, op. cit. p. 257.

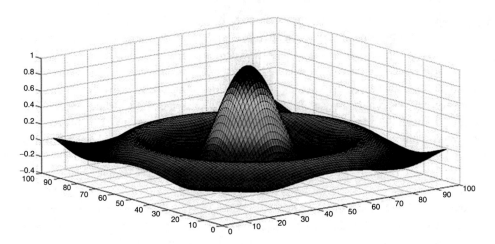

Fig. 3.2 Mexican hat function (Source: Hamid Taghavifar Coventry University)

improvement in learning accuracy. The costs associated with the labeling process can make a fully labeled training set unaffordable, while the collection of unlabeled data is relatively inexpensive. In such situations, semi-supervised learning can be of great practical value.

A special hybrid form of machine learning is also so-called "reinforcement learning". Due to its high practical relevance, a separate section is dedicated to it.

3.2.3   Reinforced Learning

Unlike supervised learning, in reinforcement learning no correct results are given and no training data is available. However, the learning process does not remain uninfluenced as in unsupervised learning, but takes place heuristically according to the "trial and error" method through positive or negative feedback during the search process. Armbruster states: "The programmed self-mortification is supposed to discipline the machine. This form of discipline and order is called 'reinforcement learning' …".[25]

Unlike the other two methods, however, reinforcement learning does not require any data in advance. Instead, these are generated and labeled in a simulation environment in many runs in a trial-and-error process during training. In reinforcement learning, the neural network thus learns through experiences made and not through specifications.

According to Gentsch, reinforcement learning belongs to the field of "exploration learning", in which a system must autonomously, i.e. apart from the directional rewards and punishments, find its own solutions or suitable output patterns, which may differ significantly from the solutions devised by humans.[26]

---

[25] Alexander Armbruster, op. cit. p. 85.

[26] See Peter Gentsch, op. cit. p. 39; Andreas Wagener, op. cit. p. 55.

Reinforcement learning thus stands for a set of machine learning methods in which an agent independently learns a strategy to maximize the rewards it receives. In this process, the agent is not shown which action is the best in which situation, but rather receives a "reward" at certain points in time, which can also be negative. Based on these rewards, he approximates a utility function that describes what value a certain state or action has.

There are various algorithms for learning the agent's strategy. Monte Carlo methods and Temporal Difference Learning are very successful in this regard (With a TD learning algorithm, an agent makes the adjustment not when it receives the reward, but after each action based on an estimated expected reward). These are a set of algorithms where the agent has a utility function that values a particular state or a certain action in a state.

For small state or action spaces, this can be a table whose fields are updated based on the reward received. However, for large state spaces, the function must be approximated.

The goal in learning is to maximize the number of rewards within a simulation environment. During training, the agent performs actions within this environment at each time step and receives feedback on each action.

Reinforcement learning is based on the basic idea of teaching a system how to minimize the punishment and maximize the reward. This is similar to supervised learning with the idea of punishing the machine when the answer is wrong. The idea is to learn optimal action rules from experience.

The use of "reinforcement learning" is particularly useful where the outcome is still open but a trend towards success or failure is already apparent.

As a result, reinforcement learning (RL) enables a form of artificial intelligence that can solve complex control problems without prior human knowledge. Compared to conventional engineering, such tasks can be solved many times faster, more efficiently and, in the ideal case, even optimally. Leading AI researchers describe RL as a promising method for achieving Artificial General Intelligence (AGI).

3.2.4   Deep Learning

The learning methods presented so far have improved AI applications in gradual stages of development. Deep learning (multi-layered, deep or deeper learning) shows an essential difference to this. Here, an explicit attempt is made to simulate the human brain.

Yet the approach is not new. As early as 1943, the mathematicians Warren McCulloch and Walter Pitts introduced the "neuron" to computer science as a logical threshold element with multiple inputs and a single output. As early as 1958, Frank Rosenblatt introduced the perceptron and thus the first, albeit very simplified, artificial neural network. Rosenblatt showed that a simple perceptron with two input values and a single output neuron can be used to represent the simple logical operators AND, OR and NOT.

According to Schmidhuber, the "father" of Deep Learning is the Russian-Ukrainian mathematician Alexey Ivakhnenko with his Group Method of Data Handling (GMDH). The development of GMDH consists of a synthesis of ideas from different areas of science:

the cybernetic concept of the "black box" and the principle of successive genetic selection of pairwise traits.

When it was claimed above that Deep Learning simulates the human brain, it must be admitted that this statement comes across as rather flippant and still needs to be specified: After all, the human brain has about 86 billion (hopefully pink!) nerve cells or neurons. The length of all nerve tracts of the brain of an adult human being is about 5.8 million km, which corresponds to 145 times the circumference of the earth. (The author may be so bold as to note here that the male brain is on average 100 g heavier and 0.14 l larger than the female brain, without this becoming apparent in terms of brain performance). These billions of neurons are connected to each other via synapses (= connection weights), which are estimated to be around 100 trillion in the human brain. Even if a quantum computer could manage this capacity (for the energy required for this, however, a forest of wind turbines would have to be available or the lights of a large city would have to go out!), a simulation of the human brain would not really be possible. The reason is quite banal: Brain research still only partially understands how the human brain works, so there cannot yet be a comprehensive replica.

In this respect, it is only true that neural networks are "modeled on the information processing units and storage mechanisms of the biological brain."[27] Ramge writes: "In ANN (author's note: artificial neural networks) and deep learning, the human brain with its neural pathways is not replicated with electronic conductors, as is often erroneously assumed. Rather, they are a statistical process in which nerve cells are simulated with so-called nodes, which are arranged in many layers behind or on top of each other."[28]

It is important to note that ANNs are not programmed, but are usually trained in a supervised manner. They consist of an input layer and an output layer, as is generally the case with machine learning. The special feature of Deep Learning lies in the middle layer, the so-called "hidden layers". This is "layered" or folded much deeper than in other machine learning.

Figure 3.3 shows a further development of the ANN, namely a Convolutional Neural Network (CNN), whose founder is Yann LeCun and whose mode of operation is explained very nicely in the following figure by Vinod Sharma from Thailand.

The structure of a classical Convolutional Neural Network consists of the visible input layer and one or more convolutional layers, followed by a pooling layer (subsampling layers).

In the input, a raw data input is processed, such as the individual pixels of an image. This input data is visible and verifiable. The convolutional layer is the actual convolutionalplatform. It is able to detect and extract individual features in the input data. Convolution applies a set of convolutional filters to the input images. Each of these filters activates specific features from the images. In image processing, these features can

---

[27] Ralf Otte, op. cit. p. 213; Alexander Armbruster, op. cit. p. 60 f.
[28] See Thomas Ramge, op. cit. p. 46.

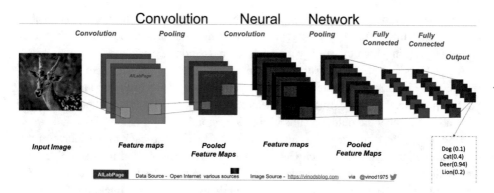

Fig. 3.3 Model of a CNN (Source: Vinod Sharma)

be such as lines, edges or certain shapes. In the pooling layer, the unnecessary information such as noise and distortions are discarded. There are different methods of pooling. By far the most common is max-pooling, where only the activity of the most active (hence "max") neuron from each neuron section of the convolutional layer is retained for further computational steps; the activity of the remaining neurons is discarded. This reduces the space requirement and increases the computation speed.

The next layer receives the information from the second layer and processes it further. These layers, which are sometimes hundreds of times on top of each other, are called hidden layers. The first layer (described in a very simplified way!) distinguishes pixels by brightness, the second layer learns to distinguish lines and shapes, the third layer recognizes more complex shapes and objects, and the fourth layer selects shapes that create a face. The contained features become increasingly abstract. Their values are not specified in the source data. Instead, the model must autonomously determine which concepts are useful for explaining the relationships in the observed data. This continues through all levels of the artificial neural network.

In principle, this process can be repeated as often as desired. With a sufficiently large number of repetitions, we then speak of Deep Convolutional Neural Networks.

This process remains hidden and cannot be traced later—it remains a "black box".

This disadvantage is mitigated by the LSTM (long short-term memory) method presented by Sepp Hochreiter and Jürgen Schmidhuber in 1997.[29] In contrast to conventional recurrent neuronal networks, this "long short-term memory" enables a kind of recollection of previous experiences: A short term memory that lasts for a long time. The LSTM method uses three types of gates to improve memory: an input gate, in which a new value flows into the cell; a forget gate, in which a value remains in the cell or is forgotten; and an output gate.

---

[29] Sepp Hochreiter, Jürgen Schmidhuber: Long short-term memory In: Neural Computation (journal), vol. 9, issue 8, pp. 1735–1780.

The final layer of the Convolutional Neural Network is the fully connected and visible layer (output), the "Dense Layer". It joins the repeating sequences of the convolutional and pooling layers, in which the strongest signals are passed on in each case.

All features and elements of the upstream layers are fully connected to each output feature (see Fig. 3.3). Therefore this output layer is also called a "fully connected layer". For this purpose, the matrix structure of the preceding "folded" layer is "flattened" in order to be able to display the output results in simple vector form.

To optimize the result, the error in the network is then traced back to the source of the error via backpropagation[30] which Geoffrey Hinton was instrumental in developing, and the gradient of each neuron is calculated and the weights adjusted in the direction of the steepest slope of the error surface. This increasingly uses a "rectified linear unit" (ReLU), which projects any negative input to 0. Previously learned patterns are overwritten when new learning occurs (so-called "catastrophic forgetting").[31]

"Evolutionary computing" is also used as an alternative to backpropagation. Just as natural mutations occur in biological evolution under adaptation pressure, this approach computes an initial solution. Each subsequent generation is generated by stochastically removing less desirable solutions and introducing small, random changes. Thus, the fitness function of the algorithm increases steadily. Evolutionary computation techniques can thus generate highly optimized solutions in a wide range of problems.[32]

Deep neural networks can have a complexity of up to a hundred million individual parameters and ten billion computational operations per input data.

Compared to conventional non convolutional neural networks, the Convolutional Neural Network offers numerous advantages. It is suitable for machine learning and artificial intelligence applications with large amounts of input data, such as in image recognition. The network operates robustly and is insensitive to distortion or other optical changes. The CNN can process images captured under different lighting conditions and from different perspectives. It still recognizes the typical features of an image.

Convolutional neural networks were therefore initially used in particular for the machine processing of image or audio data, with e.g. the "ImageNet" database containing millions of images being available for "feeding" the networks, for example.

The most spectacular application is the generation of artificial content (deepfakes). For this, two systems are combined: the first (generator) generates something and the second (discriminator) evaluates the result. For example, if the discriminator is trained to recognize landscapes, the generator can learn to create images of landscapes from random input. These Generative Adversarial Networks (GANs) work so perfectly that one cannot detect the forgery of images or videos.

---

[30] See Alexander Armbruster, op. cit. p. 131 ff; Ralf Otte, op. cit. p. 240.

[31] See Peter Gentsch, op. cit. p. 37.

[32] See Andrea Wagener, op. cit. p. 58.

Despite the impressive results achieved by CNN, particularly in the area of connectivity (image, face and voice recognition), it should not go unmentioned that these networks are particularly vulnerable to attacks. The danger is referred to as "Adversarial Examples". By manipulating input signals that are imperceptible to humans, fatal miscalculations can be generated. For example, in the case of an autonomous vehicle, incorrect traffic signs could be entered, which would lead to chaos.

Nevertheless, the great advantage of the deep learning method remains that it can be used for a great deal of problems. Originally developed for image and speech recognition, these systems can now also "read" audio files, identify smells or sharpen the tactile sense of robots.[33]

For the sake of completeness, two other types of learning should also be mentioned: "predictive learning", in which an agent attempts to create a model of its environment by logically trying out different actions under different circumstances.[34] "Transfer learning," on the other hand, involves applying a successful problem solution to a similar problem. If an AI model can recognize animal images, for example, it can also be used for tumor detection, among other things.[35]

This is a very "coarse-grained" description of the main AI learning procedures. In the next sections, a few more selected technical AI problems will follow.

3.3   The Masses Do It—Big Data

Machine learning and big data are directly related. Only with the types of learning just described can the mountains of data that are constantly piling up with digitization be made useful at all.

And this mountain of data is growing exponentially: It is assumed that Google receives up to 5 billion search queries per day (!).[36] Already in 2017, the "ocean of data" grew by about two and a half exabytes per day (1 EB = one million gigabytes).[37] By 2025, it is said to have accumulated 175 zettabytes (one zettabyte = 1 trillion gigabytes).[38]

Big Data, they say, are the "golden nuggets" or the "new oil" of our era.[39] It is not the quantity but the quality of the data that makes it valuable. And it is up to the expertise of 'data scientists' to turn Big Data into 'smart data'.

---

[33] See Ulrich Eberl, op. cit. p. 102.

[34] See Andreas Armbruster, op. cit. p. 60.

[35] See Stefan Gröner/Stephanie Heinecke, op. cit. p. 136.

[36] See Katharina Zweig, op. cit. p. 84; Andreas Wagener, op. cit. p. 176.

[37] Gernot Brauer, op. cit. p. 34.

[38] See Walter Simon, op. cit. p. 82.

[39] See Peter Gentsch, op. cit. p. 1; Walter Simon, op. cit. p. 86.

In order for this "Knowledge Discovery in Databases" (KDD) to be possible at all, the "Big Five V's" must first be given:

1. Volume (mass)
2. Variety
3. Velocity (speed)
4. Validity/Veracity (data quality)
5. Value (data value)[40]

The data volume must therefore be large, whereby the claim to mass must be put into perspective. The volume must be sufficiently large compared to the total potential of the data set to be able to detect valid correlations. So the measure of "volume" is indeterminate. But the following always applies: the more data, the greater the chance of discovering patterns.

Data variety, i.e. the range of data types and sources, is also an essential criterion for successful data mining. Structured as well as unstructured data can be used. After all, "data digging" is like gold digging: you don't know whether you will find a vein, and if so, of what quality. In this respect, it is wise to define the data set as "species-rich" as possible in order to enable rich prey.

The time required (velocity) for model training and the time span until possible results are usable in practice also determine the use of data mining. Incidentally, this process can sometimes prove to be so time-consuming and labor-intensive that data mining is dispensed with, especially since massive hardware input is usually also required for data screening. Thanks to in-memory computing and grid computing, however, the computing speed is significantly increased nowadays, thus enabling the real-time analysis of extensive data sets.

Of course, it must also be checked from the outset whether the data quality (validity/veracity) in terms of validity and reliability makes data mining meaningful. The validity or relevance of the data is often difficult to assess if the data analysis is to take place in an open-ended manner. Veracity, i.e. the reliability or correctness of the data, is easier to assess. It can usually be influenced by the data analyst before the creation of the input space or the "enabler layer", as will be shown later in the description of the mining process. By the way, sometimes it is more convenient to have a large amount of fuzzy data than a limited amount of accurate data.[41]

Before data analysis, the data value is also not always easy to judge. It "resembles an iceberg floating in the sea." Only a small part is visible at first, the larger part below the

---

[40] See Peter Gensch, op. cit., p. 43 ff; Katharina Zweig, op. cit., p. 85; Gernot Brauer, op. cit., p. 33; Manuela Lenzen, op. cit., p. 43.
Andreas Wagener, op. cit., p. 39.
[41] See Kenneth Cukier, p. 46 f.

surface remains hidden.[42] Or as the philosopher Lenzen puts it: "Often the most important things are those we don't even know we don't know".[43] In addition, sometimes after the first data mining, a further, additional utilization or analysis of the data becomes apparent, or it is dug out of the "data graves" later.[44]

Once the "BIG V's" have been established as sufficiently given, it is necessary to ask how the process of knowledge extraction should take place. Unlike in classical empirical social research, no hypothesis framework or theoretical models are necessary for digital data analysis.

Otte proposes the following reference procedure for data mining:

1. Create a Business Understanding (Get a understanding of tasks and processes)
2. Data Understanding (View and understand the data)
3. Data Preparation (Prepare, clean and transform the data)
4. Modelling (Create models and generate knowledge)
5. Evaluation (Interpret the results)
6. Deployment (implement everything in the process)[45]

Many companies have an unmanageable data lake "on their doorstep". It would not be very efficient to simply fish there. Instead, it is first necessary to consider which competitive advantages could be generated with big data analytics. Possible fields of application and project goals should be compiled in this phase.

Subsequently, "data ninjas" sift through the mass of data from a wide variety of data sources with the aim of using it to gain a better basis for making decisions about their own business activities.

Then the data must be prepared in a "readable" manner. In doing so, it is important that "noisy" data is cleaned, e.g. unreliable or quite obviously irrelevant data is removed from the data dump.[46]

Einstein once said, "Information is not knowledge." Therefore, it is necessary to convert the raw data into valuable knowledge. This requires experts to realize the transfer with modern digital technology. In recent years, a whole new class of extremely powerful technologies and programs has emerged for this purpose. The focus is on open source software frameworks such as Apache Hadoop, Spark (framework for cluster analyses), NoSQL databases ("Not only Structured Query Laguage") and, for example, Map Reduce (programming model). Hadoop is based on the MapReduce algorithm generated by Google in combination with suggestions from the Google file system. Users can employ this program to process large amounts of data (petabyte range!) as part of intensive computing

---

[42] Ibid, p. 131.

[43] Manuela Lenzen, op. cit., p. 76.

[44] See Viktor Mayer-Schönberger/Kenneth Cukier, op. cit. p. 129.

[45] Ralf Otte, op. cit., p. 327.

[46] See Katharina Zweig, op. cit. p. 85.

processes on so-called computer clusters; this process is also known as cluster computing. For data sets from websites and blogs, "crawling" (methodical tracing of web documents) or "tagging" (assignment of various contents to certain keywords) is an adequate method. For offline media, "parsing" (automatic reading) is used.[47]

Once the results of digital data processing are available, they must be interpreted by "data intermediaries" in an application-oriented manner. As a rule for KDD, correlation, cluster or regression analyses or other classifications are available for this purpose. It should be emphasized that the correlations found only represent statistically valid interdependencies without proving causalities. There are a number of statistically valid but causally absurd correlations such as the correlation between margarine consumption and divorce rates, the correlation between mozzarella sales and doctorates in civil engineering, or the correlation between storks and babies. Even such interdependencies, which at first appear to be quite outlandish, can help to discover conclusive causalities behind them via third-party variables. For example, storks and babies correlate with the independent variable "rural population", which begets more children than urban dwellers. Therefore, the results must always be checked for plausibility without prejudice in order to implement successful applications from them. In this context, demonstrable causality is not essential for the implementation of the results of data mining. Banally stated: With petabytes of data volume, correlation is enough! Thus, it was discovered through data mining that not only the cancer cells themselves, but also the healthy cells in the vicinity have a significant influence on the course of the disease, without the reason being known to this day. The numerous applications, some of which have resulted from astonishing correlations, often truly coincidental, will be reported in detail in Chap. 4.

But this much can already be said: datafication will not only continue to advance in commerce and industry, but is increasingly affecting all areas of life, so that precautions must be taken to ensure that we preserve our "digital dignity".[48] However, the author has little confidence that the EU Digital Charter can really protect us. It is true that its preamble states, among other things, that human dignity is inviolable even in the digital age and that profiling by public authorities or private individuals is only permitted on a legal basis. It also states that everyone has the right to live freely and unobserved in their own home. Google, Facebook or Amazon will only smile about that. When the author "googled" Nanjing yesterday because of a guest professorship offered to him there, booking.com already emailed him half an hour later with hotel offers for the old Chinese imperial city. All of us know the ad, "Customers who bought this also bought . . .". Unabashedly, Google boasts, "We know where you are. We know where you've been. We can more or less know what you're thinking right now."[49] The extent to which the "datafication of social life"[50]

---

[47] See Peter Gensch, op. cit. p. 75.

[48] See Andreas Wagener, op. cit. p. 240.

[49] See Walter Simon, op. cit. p. 85.

[50] Andreas Wagener, op. cit. p. 257.

has progressed is demonstrated by Michal Kosinski of Stanford, who claims for his software that with ten Facebook likes it can assess a person better than his work colleague, with 70 likes it can also assess him better than his friends, and with 300 signals it can assess the person better than his partner(s).[51] The futility of the demand of Big Data ethics to empower the individual to shape informational freedom and data sovereignty,[52] was exposed by Steve Jobs when he replied in an interview to the question why there had been no market research for the iPad: "It's not up to the consumer to know what he wants."

This attitude, which signals a social upheaval through AI, is charmingly described as "Customer Relationship Management" (CRM). Algorithms do not always successfully link in the customer's interest, as the following real-life example shows: In a very respected family, they unexpectedly and certainly unintentionally dampened the Christmas spirit mightily. The elderly father of the family had probably—bypassing his wife—freshened up his love life a little and supplied the corresponding lady lavishly with sexy lingerie via Amazon. In the sense of "personalized advertising" Amazon had sent the wife a gift box with the same underwear as a small thank you for Christmas. The husband reportedly had quite a bit of trouble explaining to his wife why the gift had turned out to be two sizes too small. Here, the neurons had obviously "fired" incorrectly at a synapse and neglected the criterion "customer age". Otherwise, the algorithm would have set the probability that the elderly customer would buy his wife sexy lingerie to less than 1. But AI algorithms just don't have any life experience yet. That's why the sentence of the late FAZ editor Frank Schirrmacher "Man is becoming the sum of his algorithms." has so far only limited application.

This is in no way to deny the advantages of the progressive data graphization of our lives. In Chap. 4—quite the contrary—countless examples will show how AI makes our lives easier and more interesting. But before that, one aspect of data mining needs to be addressed in a mainstream way.

The question arises whether the mobile phones of the "Friday for Future" youths emit less particulates than the passing SUVs that are being demonstrated against. The energy consumption by Big Data and its mining has probably never been calculated exactly. But it's certainly so high that we can't actually afford it because of climate change, unless AI also offers us alternative energy resources soon. The digital trail that each of us leaves behind is already flooding the data silos with our "data exhaust".[53]

---

[51] See Wu Youyou, Michal Kosinski, and David Stillwell, Computer-based personality judgments are more accurate than those made by humans, 2015.

[52] See Andreas Wagener, op. cit. p. 234.

[53] See Viktor Mayer-Schönberger/Kenneth Cukier, op. cit. p. 143.

3.4   Yota-Bites and Qbits—Hardware for AI

The complex AI techniques described in the last sections naturally require corresponding hardware, the development of which will be discussed in this section.

The author still remembers how he "pierced" sets of punched cards with a metal rod in the 1960s in order to be able to read out crosstabs on punched tape for his diploma thesis. During his internship abroad at a French bank, he saw a computer for the first time—he was led by the bank director himself with solemn gestures into a chilly room, where metal columns resembling armored cabinets hummed menacingly in his face. Nowadays, any mobile phone owner would sneer at the computing power performed there. But at the beginning of the 80s, we slide rule experts were also proud to own a Commodore 64 with a memory of 64 KB (!) and enthusiastically played ping-pong on the "Pong console" of the Atari 800 XL, whereby it did not bother us that the "balls" were only strokes, because they could already be "directed" with a joystick (see Fig. 3.4).

At the Cebit 1986, the author, as head of the media laboratory of the University of Applied Sciences Würzburg-Schweinfurt, was able to get hold of a head-set at the special university price of 500,000 DM (= 250,000 €), which was so heavy that it would have justified a hefty increase in his health insurance policy. But at least it was used to produce a virtual assessment center for Siemens AG, which the young engineers there enthusiastically tested. Back then, when the author was already talking about easily portable data glasses and emotional-modular wallpaper in his lectures, some colleagues already saw him committed to the psychiatric hospital.

This personal experience is deliberately described in order to illustrate the exponential development that hardware has undergone to date and that can still be expected in the future. After all, 64 KB has now become between 700 and 1400 terabytes (1 terabyte = 1000 gigabytes) in RAM on the most powerful computers. Titan at Oak Ridge National Laboratory, Tennesee had a RAM of 710 TBytes back in 2013 and managed 17.59 peta-flops/s (1 petaflop = 1 quadrillion computing operations per minute! (Flops = Floating Point Operations Per Second); Tianhe-2 in Guangzhou, China, already had a memory of 12,400 TB and a computing power of 33.86 petaflops/s in its first expansion stage in 2013,

Fig. 3.4 Pong console (Source: Atari Inc.)

and was surpassed as the world's fastest computer in 2016 by the Sunway TaihuLight at the National Supercomputing Center, Wuxi, Jiangsu in China with a computing speed of 93.0146 petaflops. In 2019, the top two spots were taken by the IBM-built "Summit" supercomputer with a record performance of 148.6 petaflops and the "Sierra" facility at Lawrence Livermore National Laboratory in California, which has a peak performance of 94.6 petaflops. And while these lines are being written, development has certainly progressed again in accordance with Moore's Law, according to which the number of transistors on microchips doubles approximately every 2 years. And it is getting cheaper and cheaper: 35 years ago you would have had to spend about 19 billion $ US (!) for the computing power of the "Summit"—today less than 50 $ US are enough.[54] However, the technically feasible limit for minimizing the transistor size is gradually becoming apparent. Intel was already struggling to bring the promised 10-nanometer (nm) chip to market in 2019. The single transistor on such a microchip is smaller than a flu virus. The technical minimum size for microchips, and thus the end of Moore's Law, was 5 nm just a few years ago, according to experts, because it was believed that transistors smaller than 7 nm would experience "quantum tunneling" through the gate oxide layer of the chip. (So-called quantum tunneling describes the quantum mechanical phenomenon that a particle can overcome a potential barrier of finite height even if its energy is less than the "height" of the barrier). But in the meantime, Samsung is teaming up with TSMC (Taiwan Semiconductor Manufacturing Company) to announce a 5 nm chip for its smartphone. Taiwanese semiconductor manufacturer TSMC plans to launch a 3 nm chip in 2021 and Intel promises it in 2025.

Even if the miniaturization of chips has not yet come to an end, the real quantum leap in hardware development is the quantum computer. Before discussing its computational capabilities and multiple applications, it is necessary to describe some of its essential features. What the conventional computer has in its bit, the quantum computer has in its subatomic quantum bit (qubit), i.e. the smallest memory unit. The crucial difference between the two is that bits have the state 1 or 0, whereas qubits "flicker" in an intermediate state between 0 and 1, the so-called "superposition", until they change to the value 1 or 0 by observation or measurement ("decoherence"). This is perhaps illustrated by the thought construct of Nobel Prize winner Erwin Rudolf Josef Alexander Schrödinger, the "Schrödinger Cat". In this thought experiment, the cat and an unstable atomic nucleus, which radiates with a certain probability within a certain period of time, are located in a box that cannot be looked into. Using a Geiger-Mueller counter, the radiation can trigger the release of poison gas, which would kill the cat. Schrödinger argues that—if quantum physics were also applicable to macroscopic systems—not only the atomic nucleus but also the cat would enter an unstable state. This ambivalence would only end when someone checks the cat's state. This would be an observation or a measurement, which would determine either the result "dead" or "alive". Until then, the cat would be in a paradoxical

---

[54] See Andrea Cornelius, op. cit., p. 24; Zukunftsinstitut, 2019, p. 113.

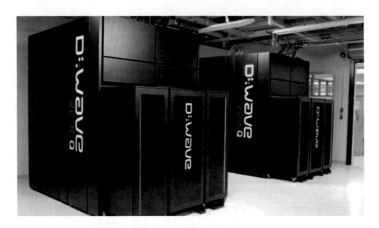

Fig. 3.5 "Quantum computer" by Wave (Source: D-Wave Systems INC)

state, namely alive and dead at the same time, i.e. in a so-called "superposition", where two physically equal quantities are in equilibrium and do not interfere with each other.

The reader surely already suspects that this diffuse "intermediate state" of the ions/photons enables the "quantum leap" in computer performance. Several qubits strung together result in a quantum register in which the elementary particles are "entangled" with each other. This means that they are in the same state mode. This entanglement can also take place between quantum registers. This is called correlation between subsystems, which can take place over long distances. The amazing thing is that with this entanglement the state of all particles changes when by measurement a part is "quantized" from the "suspended state" into 1 or 0. This happens "instantaneously", i.e. without any loss of time. This "non-locality" of entanglement and the possibility of quantum teleportation will inspire us to some speculation in Chap. 7.

The first immense advantage of a quantum computer is therefore its enormous storage capacity. Since a qubit in superposition has two states, four qubits already have 2^4 states and only 10 qubits already have 2^{10} value possibilities. The further advantage lies in its speed in computing operations through quantum parallelism, through which all computing operations can be carried out simultaneously with a single application of the quantum gate.

The quantum processor Sycamore from Google shows what a giant step this means for AI. With 53 qubits, it took 200 seconds to solve the calculation task set for it.[55] This would have taken the world's fastest supercomputer around 10,000 years. The Canadian company D-Wave produced a quantum computer with 2000 QuBits back in 2017. Figure 3.5 shows the computer cabinets for the 2000-qubit machine from 2017. In September 2020, D-Wave already offers quantum computers with a capacity of 5000 qubits.

In January 2019 at CES, IBM unveiled the world's first commercial quantum computing system that can be taken out of the IBM lab, the "IBM Q System One" with 20 qubits.

---

[55]Dpa on October 24, 2019.

Fig. 3.6 Q System One from IBM. (Source: Courtesy of International Business Machines Coporation, © (2020) International Business Machines Corporation)

These are amazing and significant advances in computing hardware. However, it must be noted that these developments do not yet allow practical use, or only very limited use. Quantum error culture still needs to be improved. To keep the superposition state stable, the machines must be set up completely free of vibration, and the qubits must be cooled to minus 273.15 °C in the superconducting quantum processor "ion trap" (in IBM's Q System One, a hermetically and airtight dilution cooling cube that is 2.8 m long and 2.8 m wide). (The square glass walls are important to reduce the footprint of the electronics of the entire system so that it can be moved/installed outside the research lab. However, the glass walls are not part of the cryogenics).

The One Q System One (Fig. 3.6) is in no way reminiscent of classical computers, but rather of the lighting fixtures in baroque castles.

It remains interesting, however, that IBM explicitly does not pursue the goal of "quantum superiority", but only assumes that certain information processing tasks can be performed more efficiently or more cost-effectively on a quantum computer than on classical computers. It remains to mention that David DiVincenzo already defined the following criteria for quantum computers in 1996, when he was still a manager at IBM:

- A scalable physical system with well-defined qubits
- The possibility of setting the qubits to a specific state initialize
- A universal set of quantum lattices
- long relevant decoherence times
- A measuring device specific to the qubits of their state is

Meanwhile, DiVincenzo is Director of the Institute for Theoretical Nanoelectronics at the research center Jülich & Co-Director of the JARA Institute for Quantum Information. Since 2019, there has been an intensive collaboration between IBM and the Fraunhofer-Gesellschaft within the IBM Q-Network in the field of quantum computing. To this end, IBM will not only make IBM Q-System One available to the members of the IBM Q-Network via the cloud, but will also install an IBM Q-System One for the first time outside the USA, in IBM laboratories in Germany (as well as in Japan as part of a partnership with the University of Tokyo).

Here, too, development will not stand still. Therefore, it can be assumed that "quantum supremacy", i.e. that the computing power of the quantum computer exceeds that of the fastest conventional transistor-based computer, will soon be achieved.

But the extent to which these devices are then used is essentially a question of energy supply. Just to illustrate the energy problem: The computer with the storage and processing capacity of the human brain would consume almost twice as much electricity as the entire human race currently does![56]

So what is the use of such enormous computing power of quantum computers?—For the time being, three fields of application are visible:

1. Since most cryptographic methods are based on encryption with prime numbers, the computing power of a quantum computer makes cryptanalysis a piece of cake. The advantage will probably first be exploited by the military and security services.
2. For pattern recognition of databases that are unmanageable for the human eye, quantum computers can offer the required performance in real time. This is where the Grover algorithm would come into its own. Like most quantum algorithms, it is a probabilistic algorithm, i.e. it gives the correct answer with a high probability, whereby the probability of an incorrect answer can be reduced by simply repeating the algorithm.
3. Quantum computers will make biochemical and quantum mechanical simulations possible. For example, the very fast movements of a protein are extremely difficult to observe or reproduce experimentally. Computer simulation can close this gap. Protein systems often contain many hundreds of thousands of atoms. Only modern high-performance parallel computers are able to calculate such movements with sufficient accuracy. Quantum-mechanically based simulations allow, for example, material properties to be calculated with high accuracy without any experimental effort.

Software and hardware as the basis for AI have thus been sufficiently described. Before the manifold fields of application are presented in Chap. 4, three technical phenomena are to be introduced, with which above all the future applications are closely connected.

---

[56] See Lawrence M. Kraus, What Should I Worry About, in John Brockmann, op. cit. p. 216.

3.5 Reliable Assistants—Bots/Robots and Cyborgs

Etymologically there is no way to explain the difference between bots and robots. Both terms derive from "robot"/"robath" (= compulsory service in the Bohemian kingdom) and the Slavic/Russian "robota/raboti" (=work) respectively. Factually, however, the differences are defined as follows: Bots are computer programs that perform certain tasks in an automated way and robots are technical apparatuses that are usually used to relieve humans of frequently recurring mechanical work.

Let us first turn to the bots, which can appear in the most diverse forms. We most frequently encounter them invisibly as "no name" bots, which act as a kind of operating system linking the various forms of information and interaction—in our mobile phones, for example. They also serve as digital opponents in computer games, "spider" as so-called web crawlers in Internet search engines, for example, to filter out spam mails or independently evaluate websites. With these functionalities, they belong to the "benign" bots that adhere to the Robot Exclusion Standards.

In contrast, the "malicious" bots are used, for example, to collect e-mail addresses for advertising purposes (spambot) or to spy out software gaps on servers for hacker attacks. They are also used as "cheats" in computer games, where they "unfairly" skip difficult game sections in multiplayer or online games by exploiting program errors with "glitches".

To counter this, programs or servers are provided with a "honeypot" (formerly also "iron box"), which simulates the network services of a computer, an entire computer network or the behaviour of a user, in order to obtain information about attack patterns and attacker behaviour.

Another bot category is the so-called "social bots", which primarily function as political opinion makers. They flood the social networks with discussion posts and news, but sometimes also with so-called "fake news". In 2016, the NDR magazine Zapp reported that social bots were used to spread political propaganda in the interests of their clients. Social bots were also allegedly used in the Brexit election campaign, as well as in the campaign for the US presidency between Clinton and Trump in 2016. For this reason, politicians are now demanding that these bots be identified as such. The Botometer (formerly "BotOrNot") is supposed to check Twitter accounts in this context to determine whether a bot or a human being is operating the account. However, it is said to have a high error rate.

More obvious are the chatbots such as the versatile Siri from Apple, the "intellectual" Cortana from Microsoft or the sales-ready Alexa from Amazon.[57] The fashionably versatile JiaJia and Xiaoice from WeChat (Fig. 3.7), which found hundreds of thousands of followers after just a few hours and now has over 40 million registered users, are particularly popular.[58]

---

[57] See Peter Gensch, op. cit. p. 99.

[58] See Andrea Cornelius, op. cit. p. 68.

Fig. 3.7 Chatbot JiaJia (Source: University of Science and Technology of China, Hefei)

Of course, the problem-oriented ELIZA by Joseph Weizenbaum from 1966 can no longer keep up with these chattering young "ladies". It is claimed that many users would have recognized the "Little Ice Cream" as an artificial figure only after 10 min. This clearly shows the progress of "conversational programming". Chapter 5 will report in detail on the use of chatbots.

Let's move on from the "language bots" to the biobots or nanobots, the tiny ones among the bots that can penetrate our bodies in nano size in order to "biopsy" them and, for example, detect and fight blood cancer cells.[59]

In addition to the classic nano-bots, there are now also nano-biobots, defined as such because they are "built" from biological tissue. Researchers at the University of Illinois have built a robot that is driven by muscle power: The actuator of the robot, which is only a few millimeters in size, consists of muscle fibers that are controlled by an electric current. The aim is to use biological components to build machines and systems for medical applications, for example.

This example shows quite well the smooth definitional transition from bot to robot, to which we now turn.

Robots can be both stationary and mobile machines and are controlled by computer programs. The (now obsolete) VDI Guideline 2860 defined robots as follows: "Industrial robots are universally applicable automatic motion machines with multiple axes whose movements are freely programmable (i.e. without mechanical or human intervention) in terms of sequence of movement and paths or angles, and are sensor-guided if necessary. They can be equipped with grippers, tools or other manufacturing equipment and can perform handling and/or manufacturing tasks."

The various types of robots are distinguished according to:

---

[59] See Jerry Kaplan, op. cit. p. 67; Klaus Mainzer, op. cit. p. 141 ff.

Construction method:

autonomous mobile robots, humanoid robots, cognitive robots, walking robots, gantry robots.

and according to **intended use**:

Exploration robot, industrial robot, medical robot, personal robot, service robot, toy robot, transportation robot, social robot.

Automobile mobile robots are one facet of hobby electronics and are often found in student competitions.

A **humanoid robot** is a sophisticated machine creature whose design is modeled on the human form. Often, the joint positions and movement patterns of a humanoid robot are inspired by human joint positions and movement patterns. Among other things, a humanoid robot usually walks on two legs. A form of humanoid robot that is particularly similar to humans in appearance and behavior is the android or gynoid(s).

A **cognitive robot** (= intelligent robot) is capable of self-perception and also perceives complex environments with rich sensors. It independently collects, evaluates and processes knowledge in order to perform meaningful actions based on this knowledge, such as creating maps or spatial concepts. Cognitive robots do not work in isolation, but in close interaction with other technical systems as well as humans and are able to improve their behavior through learning.

Walking robots are robots that can move with the help of "legs". A distinction is made here between "runners" and "crawlers". While the runners are equipped with two legs, the crawlers move with several legs, whereby six legs are the usual. The fastest of these movers is still arguably the four-legged Cheetah, first introduced by MIT in 2012. He reached a running speed of over 48 km per hour back in 2013, faster than Jamaican sprinter Usain Bolt, who only managed 45 km per hour in the 100-m dash. Since 2016, as Cheetah2, he has been able to detect obstacles via the lidar system in order to jump over them up to a height of 45 cm.

The biggest problem for walking robots is probably to keep their balance. Interesting variants of the problem solution are shown in Fig. 3.8 with Cassie from the laboratory of Jonathan Hurst at Oregon State University.

Gantry robots are actually loading or transport robots. As two-post (=half gantry) or four-post (=full gantry) linear, cantilever or area gantries, they also move heavy or large-area goods such as containers. Loading from above (e.g. via loading hatches) ensures that access to the machine is maintained. This is particularly important for set-up operations and monitoring activities on the plant.

Exploration robots primarily spy out spaces that are too dangerous or even inaccessible for humans. For example, they are used in contaminated areas, cave research, but also in space exploration.

The first **industrial robot**, the "Unimate" from the company Unimation, was used at General Motors in 1961 to remove and separate injection molded parts. Prior to this,

Fig. 3.8 Walking robot Cassie (Source: Jessy Grizzle, Robotics Institute, University of Michigan)

George Devol had applied for a patent of a programmable manipulator in the USA in 1954. In the meantime, fixed, mostly single-arm "manipulators" have increasingly been joined by mobile, sensor-equipped robots equipped with LIDAR, which work "hand in hand" with humans in hybrid work teams.

Medical robots are technical devices that are used in the medical environment and perform or assist in highly complex mechanical work. The best-known of this type of robot is probably the Da Vinci surgical system from the Intuitive Surgical company in California, which is used to perform minimally invasive operations in the urological and gynaecological fields.

A **personal robot** can be operated by a single person and is available to an individual for his or her specific needs. In this respect, there are many different fields of application for it: From reading stories to wake-up calls to style advice, everything is possible.

Service robots are divided into devices for private individuals and professional service robotics. For private households, there are tasks such as vacuum cleaning, lawn mowing or window cleaning. Professional service robots are mainly used in logistics and facility management.

Toy robots are robots that have been built as toys for children and adults. They range from simple robot figures to freely programmable, autonomous robots. In the meantime, many of these devices, such as the Dash robot and the Tinkerbots construction kit, can be controlled via smartphones.

In the sense of traffic unbundling the future belongs to **transport robots** as parcel and transport messengers. They are already being used today in industrial materials handling technology as driverless transport systems (see e.g. in Fig. 3.9). The "Smart Transport Robot" (STR) is an innovative driverless transport system (AGV) developed by the Fraunhofer Institute for Material Flow and Logistics IML together with the BMW Group as part of the "BMW Enterprise Lab for Flexible Logistics". The STR can autonomously transport boxes and is the first driverless transport vehicle (AGV) in which components from the automotive industry are installed.

Fig. 3.9 BMW Smart Transport System. (Source: BMW AG "Smart Transport Robot" (STR))

Social robots can appear humanoid and non-humanoid. Kismet from MIT was already able to recognize and simulate emotions in the 1990s. Advances in affective computing have significantly increased the functionality of these machines. Arguably the best known humanoid robot, the French/Japanese Pepper is called "Kawai" in Japanese, where "Ai" (愛) stands for "love". Pepper is already used in tutoring and the seal "Rabo" is a popular and low-maintenance house "animal" in Japanese old people's homes.

It is not by chance that the Japanese are so unreservedly opposed to robots. It is probably explained by Shintoism, in which the material world is also granted a "soul/conscious-ness". People from western cultures have more problems with acceptance. The Japanese roboticist Masahiro Mori described this in 1970 as the "phenomenon of the uncanny valley" ("uncanny valey"). It describes the correlation between human-like robots and their acceptance by users. This relationship is not steady; rather, it drops off abruptly after a certain level of anthropomorphism and only rises again after a certain, very high level. Studies show: Acceptance is highest when the imitations can no longer be distinguished from real humans at all (see Fig. 3.10).

In the case of robots, we ended with androids, thus constructing an elegant thematic transition to cyborgs. While the boundaries between bots and robots are fluid, there is an essential difference between them and cyborgs. Cyborgs are not apparatuses, but humans with "AI supports", as Fig. 3.11 impressively demonstrates.

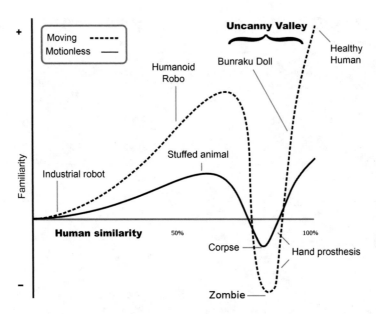

Fig. 3.10 Uncanny Valley. (Source: Jonathan Haas Uncanny Valley after Masahiro Mori and Karl MacDorman)

Fig. 3.11 Cyborg Neil Harbisson (Source: Lars Norgaard)

Fig. 3.12 Biohacker (Source: Ryan O'Shea, Grindhousewetware)

The term "cyborg" refers to a hybrid of living organism and machine. It is used to describe people whose bodies have been permanently supplemented by artificial components.

Avant-garde artist Neil Harbisson is considered the first of these cyborgs. He is the first person in the world with an implanted antenna in his skull. His antenna uses audible vibrations to give him information. This includes measurements of electromagnetic radiation, phone calls, music, and videos or images translated into sounds. His Wi-Fi antenna also allows him to receive signals and data from satellites.

"The term "cyborg" combines the words "cybernetics" and "organism". In 1960, the inventors of this composite, the two physicians Manfred Clynes and Nathan S. Kline, used it to describe the idea of the smoothest possible fusion of the natural-organic body with artificial-technological elements."[60] By this definition, Goetz von Berlichingen with his Iron Hand would already be a cyborg. His said hand was indeed "artificial", but had nothing to do with artificial intelligence. In the following, however, we will limit ourselves only to cyborgs that have AI-inspired additions. So wearers of glasses or people with headphones fall through the cracks here! It has to be parts that "get under your skin", to speak with Spreen (see Fig. 3.12).[61]

A good example of this is the cochlear implant (CI), a hearing prosthesis for the deaf and deafened whose auditory nerve is still functional as a partial organ of auditory perception. The CI system consists of a microphone, a digital signal processor, a transmitter coil with magnet and the actual implant, which is made up of another magnet, a receiver coil, the stimulator and the electrode array with the stimulation electrodes.

---

[60] Dirk Spreen, Der optimierte Mensch, in: Kultur und Technik, 4/2014, p. 27.

[61] Dirk Spreen, Cyborgs und andere Technokörper, Ein Essay im Grenzbereich zwischen Bios und Techne, 2nd edition, Passau, 2000, p. 28.

In this sense, the "self-trackers" or "lifebloggers" who come from the "quantified self movement" are not cyborgs, because the webcams or tracker bracelets used for this are not "fused" with the body. But there are isolated "self-enthusiasts," as Morozov would call them,[62] who have chosen a hybrid lifestyle for their self-monitoring, like Tim Cannon, who uses an implanted thermometer to constantly measure his body temperature and send it to his smartphone.

Even the people who use so-called "brain-computer interfaces" (= computer-brain interface) are not actual cyborgs, because they use EEG hoods and not brain implants. But cyborgization is obviously going there: experiments on the hippocampus of rats have proven that neuronal prostheses are possible. At Berlin's Charité hospital, research is being conducted into neural prostheses that are intended to improve movement after strokes and in Parkinson's patients.[63] Prostheses that are controlled by nerve signals are already in use, which will be reported on in the next chapter.

In Chaps. 2 and 3, the soft- and hardware-technical framework for the "weak" AI was outlined—hopefully in layman's terms. After the reader has eaten his way through all the "technical stuff", his curiosity must now be satisfied and a detailed report given on what can currently be done with AI.

---

[62] See Evegeny Morozov, op. cit. p. 397.
[63] See Nick Bostrum, op. cit. p. 74.

How Is AI Being Realized?: AI Determines Our Lives

4

Often the future is here before we are ready for it.
John Steinbeck

AI is the "game changer", so it is now being said everywhere. And indeed, it is already apparent that AI will intervene in all areas of our lives. This chapter reports on examples of applications that have already become socially concrete. However, the central areas of AI, "Marketing/Sales" and "Industry 4.0", are then dealt with in separate chapters.

4.1 "Big Brother" Is Not Just "Watching": Ubiquity of AI in Everyday Life

Most people are probably not even aware of how much AI is involved when they switch on their smartphone. But whether you use it to "WhatsApp", the GPS Navigator or Mobile TV and the like, it wouldn't work without the AI algorithms.

And when we google, tweet or communicate via Facebook, "Big Brother" is of course there. No sooner have you found out about a city on the Internet than booking.com makes hotel suggestions without asking. A guileless purchase at Amazon leads to an AI-induced bombardment with product-related offers.—We can no longer escape AI—it is now ubiquitous. But why should we run away from it either? We can simply click away from the unsolicited offers. Whereby the author gladly admits that many times a book recommendation has been very helpful to him. Instead of fighting back against AI with "Germanophobia" (in vain anyway), we should rather grasp the opportunities that AI offers us to make our everyday lives easier.

© Springer Fachmedien Wiesbaden GmbH, part of Springer Nature 2021
G. Cisek, *The Triumph of Artificial Intelligence*,
https://doi.org/10.1007/978-3-658-34896-0_4

Because they are increasingly shaping the everyday life of the "Generation Z" or the "Digital Natives", the chat bots sprouting from the ground will be discussed again here.

The best-known bot in Germany is probably Alexa from Amazon, which as "Amazon Echo" executes commands such as: "Alexa please* play song X", takes over the alarm clock service, answers quiz questions as a reference book and completes the shopping list on command. There are now 3000 "skills" available with the Alexa Skills Kit (ASK). And Amazon Prime customers can use Alexa to order Amazon products online, cancel them, or track their shipping. The "please" can be omitted when ordering, of course. Alexa, however, now uses "please," "thank you," and other courtesies more frequently, supposedly to counteract the brutalization of human conversation.

Duplex—a software development from Google is so linguistically adept that it was able to make an appointment at the hairdresser without the recipient realizing they weren't talking to a human.

Siri is a voice assistant for Apple devices. Siri can call or send messages for the user when they are driving or have their hands full. And Siri can make predictive suggestions, like notifying someone if you're running late for a meeting. For the visually impaired and blind, Siri reads and writes tweets. With the addition of "HomeKit," you can also turn on lights, turn up the heating, and activate the TV. The Korean version to this is called Nugu with similar functionality. Jibo, the first family robot, which—financed via a crowdfunding project—came onto the market in 2017, was also able to do all this, but was unsuccessfully shut down again in 2018.

Like Google Assistant, Alexa or Siri, Cortana from Microsoft also acts as a personal assistant with a phenomenal memory that knows what the weather will be like, when the favorite restaurant is open or where special offers are available. She also has all the appointments in her "head" to remind the user—in other words, a perfect digital secretary. Microsoft's other chatbot called TAY wasn't that perfect. It had to be shut down after just 18 h because of suggestive or insulting tweets.

Microsoft has had more success with Xiaoice, the Chinese version of a chatbot. It already has over 600 million users in China and Japan, whom it not only helps with shopping advice, but also sings, writes poetry and reads children's books to them.

While the little ice princess, who is called Rinna in Japan, still flirts disembodied, JiaJia, who was developed at Hefei University, is already an embodied chat bot. She can bat her eyelashes seductively, but still seems a bit dim-witted compared to Siri or Cortana. Her English also has room for improvement. But at least the author, who has been trying in vain to improve his Mandarin for years, fully understands that. JiaJia, this Chinese entertainment robot created by Professor Chen XiaoPing is considered "ultra-lifelike." Her still rigid face resembles that of ladies who have gone a bit overboard with plastic surgery, but she already turns quite coquettishly to the side when confronted with photographers and exchanges many a salacious comment with her "lord" XiaoPing.

Her western counterpart "Scarlett Johansson", "tinkered" by Hong Kong graphic designer Ricky Ma, already manages facial expressions, but seems rather creepy when winking.

Sophia, the robot woman from Hanson Robotics says about herself, "My AI design is based on human values such as cleverness, kindness and compassion. I want to become an empathetic robot". She explains her supposedly "expressive" face by saying that she wants to live and work with humans. Therefore, she said, she needs to express emotions in order to understand people and build trust with them. However, when asked if she wanted to kill humanity, she answered with a startlingly honest "Yes!". After all, she has 62 facial expressions at her disposal and Saudi Arabian citizenship since 2017, which she was awarded in Riyadh at the Future Investment Initiative conference.

Thematically related to the entertainment robots described here are the gaming computers such as Hydra, currently supposedly the most powerful chess computer, which brought down its predecessor "Brutus" from the company ChessBase because of poor performance. IBM's "Deep Blue"remains unforgotten, as it was the first computer to succeed in beating the then reigning world chess champion Garri Kasparov in a game with regular time controls back in 1996. In 1997, Deep Blue won an entire contest of six games against Kasparov under tournament conditions. Kasparov did not want to grant him this grandiose victory and accused IBM of having used "natural AI" to help him during the game. IBM refused the demanded revenge and angrily dismantled the $five million Deep Blue, the parts of which now rest in the Smithsonian Museum in Washington.

Even more complex was the computer program AlphaGo based on neural networks, which exclusively plays the traditional ancient Chinese board game Go. It was developed by Google DeepMind. In March 2016, AlphaGo beat South Korean Lee Sedol, one of the world's best professional players.

The first computer game "Pong" has already been reported. In the meantime, computer games have become a remarkable economic factor. In Germany alone, the annual turnover is almost five billion euros. In addition to the single-player variants, in which the game situation is only influenced by the player himself and the bot opponent (computer), there are the increasingly popular creations with a multiplayer mode, with which e-sports have developed. Even though the German Olympic Sports Confederation does not yet recognize this competition as a sport, many German sports clubs such as 1.FC Nuernberg, RB Leipzig, VfB Stuttgart and 1. FC Cologne now have e-sports departments. After all, the prize money distributed worldwide until 2019 amounted to over 780 million US dollars. The so-called "progamers" are professionals who compete against each other in tournaments ("clan wars"). The annual "World Cyber Games" are the most important event for this, with more than a million players always taking part. For e-"athletes" there are particularly powerful computer mice, keyboards, headsets or gamepads that are designed for sustained heavy use. For computer mice, there are additional aids such as Mouse Bungee, Mouse Skatez or special gaming mouse pads that improve the accuracy of the mouse movement. Of course, the pros also use powerful computer hardware, although games like League of Legends, StarCraft II, Rainbow Six and Counter-Strike can also be played on ordinary home computers.

After the "gimmicks", let's now move on to the service robots that provide a wide variety of services for us humans.

One of the oldest examples in the "cleaning robot" category is certainly the Roomba vacuum cleaner robot from the company iRobot, which has been vacuuming since 2002 and was inducted into the "Robot Hall of Fame" in 2008. Its most modern version can start on its own at a set time via a clock, vacuum around 80 m^2 in a maximum of four networked rooms and then dock back to the charging station on its own. Afterwards, "Braava", the floor-mopping robot from the same manufacturer, can wet-mop everything again. By the time the floor is shiny, it's actually too late to use "Hobot," "Mamibot" or "Pearl," three of several window-cleaning robots sprouting on the market. For animal lovers, "Lady Bird" is available as a vacuum cleaner that sucks everything dutifully, but can be equipped with the function: "I brake for animals" so that vermin survive. It will probably be a few years before AMAR from the Karlsruhe Institute of Technology (KIT) can take care of the household on its own. But already today, with 43 degrees of freedom and equipped with two "eyes" (= cameras) and six "ears" (= microphones), it can wipe the table, empty the dishwasher and open the refrigerator. The pressure sensors of his five-fingered hand are so sensitive that Amar can even grasp raw eggs without breaking them.

In addition to the "in-house dwarfs", there are also devoted servants around the house. Figaro "is very satisfactorily at my neighbour's service: an autonomous lawn mower. He shares the care outside the house with "Helios" or "Scobbi", the photovoltaic cleaning robots (see Fig. 4.1) and of course with a rain gutter cleaning robot and a robotic pool cleaner. Those whose domicile is by the sea should also treat themselves to the purchase of a beach cleaning robot (see Fig. 4.2).

And while these lines are being written, new robo-creations for further services are probably already ripening.

Just casually mentioning the obviousness that the AI-savvy household also keeps a surveillance robot to keep all the stuff on the property.

Fig. 4.1 Photovoltaic cleaning robot "Geko Solar" (Photo: Serbot AG, Switzerland)

Fig. 4.2 Sand beach cleaner (Source: Prof. Smithmaitrie, Prince of Songkla University, Thailand)

Let's leave the domestic space and look at what we encounter on the street in terms of AI in everyday life. The latest are e-scooters, which of course have a GPS module so that you can collect the things again. But this software also registers the ride history including its speed. It also determines whether the bike lanes forbidden to him were used. The Californian company Lime Bike, which offers such scooters, wants to send each user a map after the end of the ride, on which the distance covered on the pavement that is forbidden is marked.[1]

Scoffers claim that our cars are now mobile phones on wheels that have grown up. At least they are fully equipped with AI. From ABS to the navigation system, the parking aid, the automatic distance control and the lane-keeper assistant, algorithms are at work to make road traffic easier for us. Even the toll sensors for trucks and the electronic traffic guidance on motorways cannot do without AI.

In the US states of California, Nevada and Arizona, automobiles are already driving in the true sense of the word, namely as self-driving motor vehicles.[2] And in Germany, too, prototypes such as BMW's "iNext" are already ready for registration. And back in 2014, the truck manufacturer presented the Mercedes-Benz Future Truck 2025. In 2015, Daimler's "Freightliner Inspiration Truck" received road approval as the first ever partially automated commercial vehicle. It is surprising that traditional carmakers are facing serious competition from providers from outside the industry such as Tesla, Google, Bosch or ZF with "ZF Pro AI".

---

[1]Max Sellmer, Christian Hensen, Lime E-Scooter: Runter von den Bürgersteigen!, in: Computerwoche from January 29, 2020.
[2]See Ralf Otte, op. cit. p. 317.

But all vehicle suppliers have already recognized that the "mission" of the cars is changing with the autonomy of driving.[3] In addition to the transport function, the entertainment function of the vehicles is also being added. Entire departments of the most important manufacturers are already researching the subject of the "world of the car adventure", using not only designers but also sound artists, interior designers, lighting designers, scent experts, psychologists and "social spies" to track down social trends. Not quite as futuristic, but practical, is Ford's Evos Concept, in which the user's personal data cloud is already being used to guide people with pollen allergies past areas with heavy pollen counts.

At the same time, the approval of these "moving living rooms" is likely to drag on for a while, at least in Germany. In my lectures on the subject, participants repeatedly evoke the associated risk of accidents. The reference is always made to the unfortunate cyclist who—suddenly emerging from the bushes at night—was run over by a self-driving Tesla car, the only known accident victim in this context so far, which contrasts with the more than 3000 road deaths in Germany alone every year. (The question of guilt in this respect is dealt with in detail in Chap. 8) To ban these "self-driving cars" because of the problems that cannot be denied at all would be paradoxical. For the car robots, with their LIDAR system (LIDAR = laser detection and ranging) and 1.3 million data points per second[4] (including blind spot monitoring, automatic distance warning, distance control, pre-crash and pre-brake), at least have a chance to weigh things up, while the human driver, after the "second of shock", has already "thoughtlessly and willlessly" left the accident where his vehicle has thrown him. Experts believe that self-driving cars would drastically reduce the number of accidents, since 90% of accidents are currently caused by human error.[5]

The real problem for the deployment of the "car robots"is much more trivial. Before they can hit the road as a "swarm", not only must a 5G network be installed, but a much higher energy volume must also be available, because the self-driving cars eat up a lot of electricity.

This is all the more true if the trucks are to roll on the road in future in a 24-h rhythm using the platooning method, in which, among other things, the braking systems of the "elephant convoy" are also networked with each other to reduce the distance. If, on top of this, the driverless cab becomes a logistics centre[6] in which journeys are planned autonomously according to the order situation, loading and unloading are controlled autonomously and administrative tasks are also carried out on the road, many windmill forests will be necessary. Even sensible transport solutions such as car sharing and "valet parking", with which the car—without valet—looks for a parking space itself via an app from the smartphone and also returns to it when called by the user, will not be able to change much

---

[3] See Bettina Volkens, op. cit. p. 106.

[4] See Erik Brynjolsson/Andrew McAfee, op. cit. p. 71.

[5] See Ulrich Eberl, op. cit. p. 173.

[6] See Gernot Brauer, op. cit. p. 143.

about this.[7] And the electrically driven People Mover minibus, which ZF is developing for autonomous mobility in inner-city traffic, is more likely to exacerbate the problem than solve it.

Let's turn to a more socially friendly AI genre: the aforementioned social robots. One of the most popular of these is probably the artificial Japanese harp seal Paro, which is used primarily in nursing homes for therapeutic purposes with dementia patients. Also from Japan comes the robotic dog Aibo, which uses a camera and microphones to perceive and process information from its surroundings. Aibo can wag its tail and ears and roll around on the floor like a lap dog. His current version also recognizes smiles or words of praise and shows a sense of well-being when you stroke his head and back—making him a pleasant and easy-to-care-for "pet". The evolution of Aibo is called Qrio and is a homanuid robot that could hop, climb stairs, play soccer, read stories aloud, sing and also dance. He painstakingly recognized speech and faces, and with a Japanese vocabulary of 60,000 words after all, was a reasonably competent conversationalist. However, it remained only a prototype, and Sony has stopped further development of it until further notice with the halt of Aibo. Its official successor is Nao, which is now shipping in its sixth version and can, for example, take on the role of a strict fitness trainer.[8] Jibo, developed in 2013 with the help of a crowdfunding project, also had a short life until 2018, when the servers on which he was running were shut down. He was the first—almost disembodied—family robot that could display graphics and text with a display on the back of his head. Ownership of the robot doll with the comical name "My Friend Cayla," which was named "Top 10 Toy of the Year" by the German Association of Toy Retailers as recently as 2014, has been considered a criminal offense in Germany since 2017 at the urging of the Federal Network Agency because it is capable of surreptitiously recording images or sound. That concern doesn't exist with Pleo, the AI replica of a baby Camarasaurus dinosaur. Pleo crawls on all fours, can move its head and tail, close its eyelids, and open and close its mouth. Interestingly, he goes through different stages of development. At the beginning he mimics the state of a newborn, then behaves like a child and finally like a teenager.

The probably most media-effective and so far most successful "robot companion" is called Pepper (Japanese: Kawaii) in the western world and is supplied by SoftBank with different applications, which have to be purchased.

The child-sized Pepper has two cameras and four microphones and can thus recognize faces and states of mind and respond accordingly to his counterpart. He is therefore often used as a sales consultant. But because he is programmed to be very "amiable", he is now also proving himself patiently as a tutor. He currently speaks four languages (English, French, Japanese and Spanish) and further language applications are planned. For questions that can be answered by data search, Pepper makes himself smart via the Internet. Its repertoire of gestures supposedly takes into account culture-specific peculiarities

---

[7] See Alexander Armbruster, op. cit. p. 68 f.

[8] See Manuela Lenzen, op. cit. p. 223.

Fig. 4.3 Pepper in the original
(Source: SoftBank Robotics
Europe)

between Japan and the USA. For the European culture this adaptation is obviously still missing, because during the visit of the German chancellor he refused to shake her hand and bowed constantly according to Japanese tradition. Despite this lack of culture, he was the first robot to host "Kulturzeit" on 3satTV (Fig. 4.3).

In comparison, the "Smart Toy Monkey" from Fisher Price is really just a stupid monkey. ASIMO, the humanoid robot from Honda, doesn't stand a chance against Pepper either, because it has no learning ability whatsoever and is taught everything by programmers. So he already belongs to the senior generation of robots.

In contrast, "Care-O-bot 3" from the Frauenhofer Institute IPA is a real competitor for Pepper. It has already proven itself in practical use at an inpatient care facility for the elderly. The focus was on two application scenarios for the robot: supplying residents with drinks and using it as an entertainment platform, as can be used by nursing staff as part of their daily work."[9] "Armar 3″ from the Karlsruhe Institute of Technology can boast similar quality. He prefers to help in the kitchen, where he can clean out the dishwasher, for example. With his sensitive data glove, he can also fetch cups, mugs, rice or juice packets. He also fetches drinks from the fridge and wipes down the table when called or given a hand signal. Dinsow, the Thai geriatric nurse, doesn't seem that versatile yet, but he enjoys great popularity in the Far East.[10]

---

[9] See Ulrich Eberl, op. cit. p. 186.

[10] See Stefan Gröner/Stephanie Heinecke, op. cit. p. 202.

Modern dating doesn't need social robots, it works digitally via corresponding portals like Tinder and WhatsApp. A little more sophisticated are implanted chips on which the partner preferences are stored and which give acoustic signals during encounters with other cyborgs if the partner criteria match—then it has literally "sparked".

Since the chance of finding each other this way is quite small, there are of course already social robots of a special kind: the sex robots with sometimes surprising possibilities. For example, the face of "Solana" can be skinned to transform the otherwise still rather awkward lady into a new type. In China and Japan, "female" sex robots with speech and facial expression functions as well as "body heat" are in particular use. In the Japanese sex game "Lovela × Cation" it is even allowed to marry such a virtual partner.[11] But you don't even have to travel all the way to the Far East; in Barcelona there is already a well-frequented brothel with electronic sex dolls that adapt to customers' wishes. According to a study by Bayerischer Rundfunk, Arte, ORF and the Fraunhofer Institute for Industrial Engineering (IAO), one in five Germans would like to have sex with a sex robot, and half of them wouldn't mind if their partner had such a bedfellow. In the meantime, there are already people who describe themselves as "digisexual". So far, Facebook only offers 60 (!) different gender options—"digisexual" is not yet among them. Whether such "love robots" can be used to counter the criminal side of prostitution is yet to be seen.[12] And who knows what kind of jokes the manufacturers of such substitute partners will allow themselves, thinking of the "smart" vibrators that secretly forward the "user data" to the manufacturer.[13]

AI also makes some unusual products possible. For example, there is now a smart hairbrush "Kérastase Hair Coach" from L'Oreal, which uses sensors and patent-pending signal analysis algorithms to assess the quality of the hair and monitor the effects of various hair care applications. The specially developed app is then used to make appropriately tailored product recommendations. This is naturally matched by the EBvision body mirror, which uses augmented reality software to make you look out much better than you look in, by "turning" your beer belly into a six-pack. And of course, the modern "wet room" also includes the Numi 2.0 intelligent toilet with adjustable lighting, built-in speakers and heated seats. In addition to the traditional toilet purpose, Numi also offers a personalized cleaning and drying function. Smart Fashion offers dresses that transform from floor-length evening gowns to short day dresses thanks to hidden, technical mechanisms. And Levi's is now selling a smart denim jacket that connects to a smartphone via Bluetooth and conductive thread and controls music playback and volume via the left sleeve. Sensors in the smart clothing determine the wearer's vital parameters so that an emergency call can be sent in the event of an emergency. Incidentally, a smartwatch that also functions as a

---

[11] See Holger Volland, op. cit. p. 131.

[12] See Eric Hilgendorf, in: Malte-Christian Gruber/Jochen Bung/Sascha Ziemann, loc. cit.

[13] See Britta Buchmüller, Belauscht beim Sex Smarter Vibrator nimmt Paar heimlich beim Liebesspiel, in: Kölner Stadtanzeiger, November 13, 2017.

smartphone can also do this. Deutsche Telekom is expanding its product range by selling smartties that contain love chips that prompt partners to put their cell phones aside and cuddle when they meet. The mobile phones also provide romantic music without being asked. Tonello's tJacket, which uses app-controlled airbags to simulate tender hugs, also fits the bill. The internet-enabled glasses called "Google Glass" from the class of wearables have been taken off the market again. They weren't actually glasses either, but a mini-computer attached to the side of the glasses frame.

One could continue the series of AI-influenced gadgets like this at will. But it turns out that with the enthusiasm for innovation also comes many a flop.

This is certainly also the case for some inventions in the field of "Smart Home". Emotional wallpapers, which should duly adapt to the mood of the inhabitants with colouring and design, have obviously not conquered a broad market. With qualified building intelligence, the "high-tech lingerie" can radio to the central heating system as soon as it arrives at the apartment that it should be set a little higher so that the wearer of cold underpants is quickly warmed up comfortably. The sensory "smart laundry" can also telematically program the lighting mood in the apartment and prepare a pleasant scent climate. In the meantime, in the sense of "Ambient Assisted Living", there are already floor coverings with sensors that register whether an occupant has fallen down and then trigger an alarm.[14] But we have not yet heard of any exuberant sales successes with all these innovations.

While the "smart home" is a very helpful development, especially for an aging society, AI is also blooming in some extravagant ways: At MIT, students have developed a robot garden in which every flower is a programmable robot and can bloom or change color. Moving robot sheep and robot ducks are also part of the garden, according to MIT.[15] Not only rose-growing then-Chancellor Adenauer would probably shake his head at such "virtual gardening"; but to Generation Alpha, the 3D smartphone will effortlessly replace the allotment garden, with no idea what they're missing. You don't necessarily have to buy a Bakebot either if you want to make cookies yourself, but they are available in stores.[16] Here we should also mention IBM's Chef Watson, who invites us to 'Cognitive cooking'. It knows the appropriate ingredients for any spice and compiles new recipes based on them, for which it then also provides food-technical information.[17]

With so many offers, some AI garbage naturally accumulates. For this, U. Schmid has developed the software "Dare2Del" ("Dare to delete it"), with which a "desktop messie" can clean his (hard) disk.[18]

---

[14] See Manuela Lenzen, op. cit., p. 189 f.

[15] See Martin Reche, MIT: Robot garden should inspire the next generation for computer technology, in: heise online from 20.02.2015.

[16] See Elizabeth Fish, Bakebot Robot Makes Cookies, Saves Bakers Some Work, in: PCWorld of 13 June 2011; Thomas Ramge, op. cit. p. 190.

[17] https://www.ibm.com/blogs/watson/2016/01/chef-watson-has-arrived-and-is-ready-to-help-you-cook/

[18] See Artificial intelligence to help "desktop messies", in. Star, January 13, 2020.

After all the social and love robots and amazing AI applications, the section shall end ineffectually with the humanoid Atlas robot, which I would like to call "Orang Hutan (Indonesian = forest man) sapiens" because it can roam lonely through the woods. Unfortunately, it was probably not designed just for picking berries, but, since DARPA (Defense Advanced Research Projects Agency) commissioned Boston Dynamics to make it, it is more likely to be used as a military scout in impassable or contaminated terrain.

To quickly shake off this creepy notion, we turn to a more uplifting scenario, AI in art, in the next section.

4.2 The "Virtual Mozart" Sounds Better: AI in Art

Just in time for Beethoven's 250th anniversary year, he will finish his tenth symphony—well, not really him, but a computer, or rather an algorithm, which is being "fed" by a team of six experts under the direction of Matthias Röder with the support of Telekom, so that the sketches Beethoven left to Ignaz Moschele shortly before his death were not scribbled in vain in the little red book. "The algorithm is unpredictable, it surprises us every day," said project coordinator Matthias Röder, director of the Salzburg Karajan Institute at SWR. One was therefore curious to see how the "10th of Beethoven" would sound in the anniversary year.[19] It is very doubtful whether Beethoven would have composed the tenth in this way. Processing the data set of his 8 symphonies to date would certainly not have produced his Ninth, even with the most sophisticated AI. And the idea is not new. Previously, Huawai "completed" Schubert's eighth symphony with AI, without anyone cheering the result. But that's not really the point. Rather, the project shows that technological tools can support the creative process.

The attempt to creatively combine music with mathematics is also made by Gaëtan Hadjeres as the inventor of DeepBach. He trained the computer by having it insert the missing note between bars or from entire compositions. With the gradually improved parameters, the software now composes accompanying voices and harmonies for given melodies.[20]

Back in 2015, the performance collective Gob Squad, together with the Komische Oper Berlin and the Neurorobotics Research Laboratory of the Beuth University of Applied Sciences, gave the small and one-eyed robot Myon a supporting role in the musical "My Square Lady". However, Myon disappointed his mentor, the mathematician Prof. Hild, as his "heart" did not ignite for the prima donna, but rather showed an inclination for the conductor in the orchestra pit.[21]

---

[19] See Jochen Hubmacher, Komponieren wie Beethoven, in: Deutschlandfunk, December 12, 2019.

[20] See Gaëtan Hadjereshttps, DeepBach learns to compose, in Berlin Valley, June 27, 2018; Volland, Holger, Die Kreative Macht der Maschinen, 1st ed., Weinheim, 2018, p. 92.

[21] See Ulrich Amling, Mit Schirm, Charme und Schaltkreisen, in: Tagesspiegel, June 23, 2015; Ulrich Eberl, op. cit. p. 19.

While in classical music the AI still rather tempts to music-theoretical exercises, in the light music already market-pregnant commercial interest connects itself with it.

The rap song written by an artificial intelligence of the American digital company "space150", which is musically suspiciously close to the original, the Texan singer and music producer Travis Scott (Jacques Webster), is very popular. To do this, they fed the computer with the rapper's entire discography to produce the song "Jack Park Canny Dope Man". The accompanying video is also a "deepfake" that imitates the facial features and body of the original.[22]

In 2008, Miku Hatsune became the first synthetic pop icon. She is a virtual figure with an artificial singing voice based on the software synthesizer Vocaloid2. With her seductive girlish charm, Miku probably meets the taste of the Japanese audience in particular and can now even be bought as wallpaper.

The sound engineer Alex Da Kid "composed" the song "Not Easy" based on the Watson Beat software, which analyzes the success components for hits, and it entered the rock charts right away.[23] Meanwhile, there are several services like Chartmetric or Snafu Records that use AI to guarantee the chances of success for new songs or make talent searches successful long before music-loving talent scouts can strike.[24] Cinelytic" from Warner Bros. offers something similar for the film and entertainment industry.[25]

Jukedeck offers a media library with "artificial" music with which you can accompany your videos and also an AI-controlled software with which you can generate your own soundtracks. If you give Vocaloid by Yamaha Corporation a melody and lyrics, this software synthesizer underlays both with artificial vocals that resemble the voices of real singers.

At California's Coachella music festival in 2012, rapper Snoop Dogg (real name: Calvin Cordozar Broadus Jr.) brought rapper, musician and actor Tupac Amaru Shakur, who died under mysterious circumstances, to "virtual" life when he sang a virtual duet with him as a life-size hologram.[26]

ABB's collaborative robot YuMi proves its versatility by not only working in small parts assembly, but also successfully conducting the Lucca Philharmonic Orchestra at the Teatro Verdi in Pisa, despite only having a few days of training time to do so.[27]

A rather absurd AI application is shown by the Spanish Moon Ribas. In the left upper arm of this lady is a mini-computer that accesses the Internet to register earthquakes

---

[22] Benedikt Scherm, Eine Künstliche Intelligenz schreibt einen Rap-Song, der verdächtig nah ans Original, Travis Scott, rankommt, in: SZ vom February 18, 2020.

[23] Holger Volland, op. cit. p. 88.

[24] T3n, This music label wants to find the next music star via AI, dated February 11, 2020.

[25] See Vera Tidona, Movie releases-Warner uses artificial intelligence to predict tops or flops, in Play Central News, Jan. 10, 2020.

[26] See Holger Volland, op. cit. p. 135.

[27] See automatica 2018—Professional service robotics, Smart robots conquer the service sector, in: a automation From November 23, 2017.

worldwide in real time. Depending on the magnitude on the Richter scale, Ms. Ribas dances more or less violently to spherical sounds in front of a manageable audience.[28]

Let us now move from sound to image, which is becoming increasingly important in the perceptual capacity of digital natives in the sign of the Iconic Turn, i.e. the turn towards an image science that establishes scientific rationality through the analysis of images.

In most museums, you pay a surcharge to be hung with an audio system that allows you to shimmy from exhibit to exhibit. The Heinz Nixdorf MuseumsForum (HNF) proves that it can be much more charming. Max (Multimodal Assembly eXpert), a computer-animated avatar, awaits us at the entrance as a museum guide and sometimes even engages the guests in conversation. This is made possible by the BDI architecture (B for **B**eliefs = assumptions (e.g. about the environment); **D**esires = wishes that are to be achieved/realized and the **I**ntentions = intentions for action that the agent has in order to achieve the goal), with which Max was equipped by Stefan Kopp.

Even better than a nice Max would be an "interactive" museum in which I could stylistically transform a picture by Dürer into one by, say, Cezanne at the push of a button. When I think about how verbally laborious and almost in vain the art teacher tried to teach us students the difference between Feininger's Constructivism and Picasso's Cubism, I wish she had already had at her disposal the neural algorithm for artistic style by Matthias Bethge from Tübingen, which makes it possible to edit photos in the style of famous artists.

If such a Max handed us a pair of data glasses upon entry, with which we could immerse ourselves virtually and immersively in an impressionistic summer landscape by Renoir or a battle painting by Eisenträger, our visit to the museum would be much more memorable.

What "DeepBach"is to music is "The Next Rembrandt"to painting. In 2016, with the support of Microsoft and the ING Group, a team of experts from Delft University of Technology analyzed Rembrandt's "artist DNA" by digitizing the Dutch master's portrait paintings with high-resolution 3D scanners. An algorithm examined the geometric arrangement of the faces and calculated, for example, the distances between the eyes and the nose or the distance between the nose and the mouth as well as the alignment of the eye areas. In the end, with the help of a computer program fed with Rembrandt's brushstrokes, the result was a Rembrandt that is "paradoxically more typical of him (than) any painting he actually made himself."[29]

AI-powered image-editing software gives anyone modest creativity. Adobe's machine-learning algorithm Scribbler makes black-and-white images glow with pastel colors,[30] and EyeMe lets you crop, rotate, straighten, and change perspective on photos, as well as tweak contrast, exposure, and sharpness. Luminar 4 effortlessly erases red eyes or blemished skin

---

[28] See Hakan Tanriverdi, Diese Frau vibriert, wenn die Erde bebt, in: Süddeutsche Zeitung, May 16, 2016; Manuela Lenzen, op. cit.

[29] See Madita Tietgen, 3-D printer creates a new Rembrandt painting, in: Welt, April 16, 2016; Holger Volland, op. cit. p. 56.

[30] See Oliver Nickel, Adobe Scribbler automatically colors black and white sketches, in: Golem.de from 25.10.2017.

from photos, and it turns a dull gray background into a romantic sunset on demand. It makes rotten teeth gleaming white, moon faces into distinguished thinkers' foreheads and bleary eyes become a radiantly beautiful pair of eyes by a few "intelligent" filters.

This form of image processing may not seem very artistic. But with Roman Lipski, for example, AI has already made it into famous museums around the world. In collaboration with data specialist Florian Dohmann, the Berlin-based artist has developed algorithms that are capable of generating new images on their own.[31] And for more than 400,000 US dollars, the "Portrait of Edmond Bellamy" was auctioned at Christie's in New York, which was created by an artificial intelligence on the basis of 15,000 portraits. For this, the collective "Obvious" by Hugo Caselles-Dupré, Pierre Fautrel and Gauthier Vernier had generated an appropriate algorithm. The initiative of the Frankfurter Kunstverein with the exhibition "How to make a paradise" also goes in this direction.[32]

An ordinary welding robot was turned into an artist at the University of Constance in 2013. E-David (**D**rawing **A**pparatus for **V**ivid **I**mage **D**isplay) has several cameras and a control computer. A computer program tells it which brush strokes to make and monitors what appears on the canvas. "Because the machine is capable of executing brush strokes in precise temporal sequence, e-David can be used to determine the temporal sequences in which a painting was painted. In this way, they say, it will be possible to study the painting styles of famous painters in terms of the temporal sequence in which the paint was applied. And this, the scientists hope, could even make it possible to detect art forgeries flawlessly in the future."[33]

Immediate practical application for AI arises among designers. In 2016, for example, the Elbo Chair was "artificially" designed. Arthur Harsuvanakit and Brittany Presten defined only the seat height of 18 inches and the maximum load of 300 pounds. Dreamcatcher software then developed the unusually delicate design.[34] The "A.I. Chair" by Philippe Starck, who does not even own a computer, was also developed according to his specifications for functionality in collaboration with the US software manufacturer Autodesk.[35]

Even though one might call such a thing "computational creativity", it remains to be said that the creative impetus is still a human one.

In the spirit of Iconic Turn, let us add another figurative AI aspect: "virtual reality (VR)", which could also be called "unreal reality". The immersive possibilities of visiting museums have already been briefly outlined. But what possibilities would VR offer in

---

[31] See Katrin Tobies, Roman Lipski on art and AI, in: Berlin.de of October 24.10.2018.

[32] See Rudolf Schmitz, Künstliche Paradiese?, in: Deutschlandfunk, April 04, 2020.

[33] Rainer Schuldt, e-David: Roboter als Kunstmaler, in: ComputerBild of October 30, 2013; see Manuela Lenzen, op. cit. p. 122.

[34] See Paul R. Daugherty/H. James Wilson, Human + Machine, Artificial Intelligence and the Future of Work, Munich, 2018, pp. 150 and 156.

[35] See Katharina Cichosch, Diesen Stuhl hat ein Computer entworfen, in: Spiegel vom February 17, 2020.

history classes, for example. I remember mentioning during a lecture: "Three, three, three" and the chorus of those present spontaneously adding: "at Issos Keilerei (barney)". But when I asked why Alexander had won the battle, the audience failed to answer. If they had "experienced" the battle with data glasses as Greek mercenaries of the Persian army, they would have remembered that the coward Darius had run away at times and so his army despaired without leadership.—With VR, people today could already forgo long-distance travel—for the sake of the climate—and experience tourist hotspots virtually. Soon there will be VR experiences that are not even possible in real life, such as hurtling through space at the speed of light. But beware! Our brains are amazingly easily fooled and respond to virtual images with real psychosomatic reactions. I myself have experienced how it choked me when I, clearly aware that I was only sitting in a cave (Automatic Virtual Environment), virtually hurtled down a roller coaster.

But not only VR offers new worlds of experience. AI also offers interesting possibilities for so-called "simulated reality", as it can enrich the hypothetical environment perceived as real in detail. The degree of immersion can become so intense that the simulated reality becomes VR and the subject can no longer distinguish between simulation and VR. If unreal objects are then introduced into the simulated reality, which is easily possible with AI, the so-called mindfuck is given, which can cause cognitive dissonance.

Before things get too miraculous, let's turn to the art of AI in language. Probably the most common AI application that we encounter every day and that we cannot escape is the "predictive keybord", which, for example, tells us the words before we have them "on the tip of our tongue" when typing a text message.[36] In 1911, Maria von Ebner-Eschenbach still wrote: "The spirit of a language reveals itself most clearly in its untranslatable words." The accuracy of this bon mot is sometimes amusingly proven by DeepL or Word's text check with absurd word suggestions. Despite such bloopers, one must confess that the AI language assistance is amazingly advanced. It helps Katrin Pasig with "co-writing"[37] and many business reports and fact-based articles are already written by computers today. Even entire novels are already being produced by robots.[38] It is not without reason that the Axel Springer Akademie is the first journalism school to include AI in its curriculum. One still remembers how fiercely journalists resisted when they were supposed to do the typesetting work themselves. Now they will have to get used to only smoothing out AI-produced texts.[39]

---

[36] See Alan Henry, How predictive keywords work (and how you can train yours better), in: lifehacker, 10.08.2014.

[37] See lecture "Typing robot hands", in: Saarbrücker Zeitung from December 4, 2019.

[38] See Adrian Lobe, Will robots soon be writing novels?, in Lobe's Digital Factory, February 7, 2017.

[39] See Rolling Stone, Even more digital: Axel Springer Akademie becomes the first journalism school to embed artificial intelligence in its curriculum in: Rolling Stone, February 5, 2020.

The start-up company Ella is already developing an AI that is supposed to write texts for screenplays,[40] and at the Landestheater Linz the AI is making its debut with the premiere of "Prometheus unbound". An artificial performer "GPT-2", fed with 40 gigabytes of data, takes over the linguistic leadership alongside two actors on the basis of words called out to it, from which it develops texts that its two stage partners have to respond to unprepared. This unusual play is staged by Marcel Karnapke and Björn Lengers as the artists' collective "Cyperräuber" (Cyberbandits), who want to find out whether AI can do art.[41]

The so-called "narrative science" has spawned a new branch of science: "culturomics". With the help of an online Google tool, researchers at Harvard University systematically search books for terms in order to uncover cultural trends. For example, the word "God" appears much more frequently in the first half of the nineteenth century than before or since. But the culturomics also document when censorship intervened in which country.[42]

It should be common knowledge that by now most business and sports reports are largely or even entirely generated by "AI authors", i.e. without human input. But in the meantime, one has gone one step further: In 2019, Springer Nature Verlag published the first machine-generated science book "Lithium-Ion Batteries: Basics and Applications", whose accompanying software was developed by the team for applied computational linguistics around Prof. Chiarcos from Goethe University Frankfurt.[43]

One last perspective of AI in art is to mention its use in monument preservation and archaeology. 3D and 360° technology enables the precise digitization of historical buildings, churches or monuments, which can then also be virtually walked through. In cooperation with the University of Bamberg, Coburg University of Applied Sciences offers a master's degree course in "Digital Monument Technologies" specifically for this purpose.

With the help of the "IBM PAIRS GEOSCOPE" platform, another previously unknown figure was discovered in 2019, measuring approximately 2 by 5 m and resembling a human figure. These shaded images, icons of the ancient Peruvian Nasca culture, are only visible from the air. The neural network was first trained with data from already known Nazca lines and then identified the previously undiscovered geoglyph.[44] With the Rovina technique, remote-controlled cameras explore inaccessible catacombs and caves.[45]

We have reported extensively on AI applications in art. But without bread, it remains breadless art. That is why we are now turning to "cognitive farming".

---

[40] See Steve Haak, Ein Textgenerator soll Drehbuch für Fernsehfilme schreiben, in: Gründerszene vom January 21, 2020.

[41] See "Prometheus unbound": Artificial intelligence writes text live on stage, in: Der Standard of December 9, 2019.

[42] See Martin Amrein, Was ist Kulturomik, in: Berner Zeitung, January 5, 2011.

[43] See Jan Schwenkenbecher, Die Schreibmaschine, KI als Wissenschaftsautor, in: Forschung Frankfurt, Heft 1.2020.

[44] See Peru researchers discover new Nazca lines, in Kleine Zeitung, November 22, 2019.

[45] Luciano Bordini, Artificial Intelligence for Cultural Heritage, Cambridge, 2016, p. 125.

4.3   The Unbiblical Multiplication of Bread: AI in Agriculture

In many a schoolbook, plough horses still pull the plough steered by the farmer behind them, while next to them, headscarf-adorned peasant girls tie golden sheaves. Just 50 years ago, this would have been an image of reality. Today it is only idealized nostalgia.

In the meantime, zeros and ones have become the central tools for modern farming. The digital revolution in the field and in the barn is rapidly gaining ground. Smart farming is the future! Cloud-based software, wireless sensors and digital maps have long been in use to increase agricultural yields for the growing world population.

Major agricultural machinery manufacturers have been early adopters of digitizing their equipment. John Deere is currently developing the GridCON, a line-guided agricultural machine that is supplied with electrical energy by means of a 1000-m cable that rolls up and down autonomously in a large drum while driving. This can be used to cultivate a field area of up to 16 ha. A central computer calculates the ideal track after the working area has been precisely mapped with GPS data beforehand.

Today, autonomous seed drills are already available for digital arable farming, which spread the seed at optimized distances and thus minimize consumption. The ExactEmerge seed drill, for example, can place seeds with centimeter precision at a maximum speed of 16 km/h.

In principle, "digital farming" is characterised by the principle of "single-plant" arable farming or site-specific cultivation, so-called "spot farming". For example, on the Schickelsheim domain in the Helmstedt district of Lower Saxony, a tractor equipped with sensors recognises the nutrient content of the plants by the colour of the leaves and can thus dose the fertilisers in a differentiated and precise manner. The AI-controlled hoe there knows how to distinguish sugar beets from weeds and thus removes the latter without using pesticides.

The Agro Innovation Lab (AIL) of BayWa AG and RWA Raiffeisen Ware Austria AG held an agricultural robot competition in April 2019, which brought interesting innovations to light. For example, the Dutch company Cerescon presented its "Sparter", an asparagus harvester that uses sensors to sense the ripe asparagus on the surface and, if it has reached the minimum size, harvests it on up to three rows simultaneously. In the process, between 19 and 23 sensors push their way through the earth, depending on the width of the dam. Each sensor emits a current. If the current flows through an asparagus spear, a stronger current arrives on the other side—because white asparagus consists mainly of water and therefore has a higher conductivity than soil. As a result, the sensor detects the position of the asparagus and passes it on to the harvesting knife. It also finds low-lying spears that a harvester would only discover 2 or 3 days later below the surface.

By the way, the robot is now also available for green asparagus from the Bremen Centre for Mechatronics (BCM).

Tensorfield from the USA offered autonomous robots for thermal weed control in row crops using heated food-grade rapeseed oil. Norway's Saga Robotics presented modular robots for UV treatment against mildew and for autonomous harvesting of strawberries. Aachen University of Applied Sciences developed the "Etarob" for the competition for selective weed control based on electro-physical principles, which can be used in any weather conditions and also at night. In the future, it should also be able to harvest potatoes and iceberg lettuce autonomously.[46]

Autonomous harvesters for apples and gooseberries have been around for some time. These fruits can be shaken or jogged so that they fall from the stem and can then be picked up. Strawberries, on the other hand, have to be picked. The company "Agrobot" from Huelva has developed a harvesting machine for this purpose, which works with gripper arms to which collecting baskets are attached, in which the fruits are cut off with knives as soon as the basket encloses the strawberry.

The robot has also long since found its way into viticulture. The "Wall-Me" prunes the vines and harvests the grapes even on steep slopes. Phenobot", which was constructed by the Julius Kühn Institute (JKI) for Vine Breeding in Siebeldingen in cooperation with the Geisenheim University of Applied Sciences, is supposed to facilitate and dramatically shorten the time-consuming and tedious vine breeding. Its task is to phenotype or determine the externally recognisable plant characteristics. On the basis of the images taken by it, phenotypic characteristics such as the formation of the flowers and yield can be assessed.[47]

Only the cucumber harvest is still a problem. Here, so-called human "cucumber flyers" without AI are still in use, because obviously identifying the green cucumbers among the green foliage is a particular sensory challenge.

The digital revolution is increasingly changing agriculture. Drones and satellites help farmers to optimize their work, they generate millions of relevant data. Today, satellites already enable the analysis of a given soil area with a resolution of 30 cm. And the evaluation of highly precise data of a current cropping period, compared to those from previous years, makes it possible for farmers to take necessary measures in time to avoid crop losses.[48] With geo-image data from TerraLoupe, for example, arable land is automatically evaluated. With SCADAfarm it is possible to optimize irrigation remotely. Precise weather data is used to determine harvest times, going so far as to increase the speed of the combine harvester when rain is imminent. And when the grain tank fills up, the truck is automatically ordered for removal.[49]

---

[46] Eva-Maria Hommel, The harvesting robots are coming, in. heise online August 15, 2018.

[47] Silvia von der Weiden, So verändern Roboter den Weinanbau, in: Welt vom September 15, 2015.

[48] See The networked field, Digital revolution: More efficient agriculture and secure harvests in: Bayer's research magazine research.

[49] See Gernot Brauer, op. cit. p. 147.

Of course, AI methods are not limited to agriculture, but are also used in livestock farming. For example, Alibaba has developed an AI that detects pregnant sows after just three days, whereas a farmer only notices this around 3 weeks after fertilisation.[50]

Modern milking robots surround the cow's teats fully automatically with their suction nozzles after the computer has registered the specific udder shape of each individual cow. Since the robot also stores important vital data of the cow in addition to the quantity and quality of the milk, diseases can be detected at an early stage.[51] Automatic feeders are of course part of everyday life in Agriculture 4.0. What is new is that automatic image processing is used to observe and evaluate the social behavior of the animals. For example, the distance between pigs tells us whether the barn is too warm or too cold.[52]

AI is also being used in vertical farming, which is intended to enable the production of plant and animal products in cities in multi-storey buildings (farmscrapers). Especially vegetables, edible mushrooms and algae can be found in the assortment of urban farming. In the "vertical farm", the water and nutrient supply is optimally regulated via sensors, without having to fear weather-related harvest failures. Vincent Callebaut's visions (see Fig. 4.4) show that, in addition to ecological benefits, there are also aesthetic advantages for urban development.[53]

The growing population and increasing level of urbanization will boost the trend towards urban agriculture. In Singapore, there is already an agricultural skyscraper from which you can really get your vegetables "regionally" and not "globally". And "sky farming" is already being successfully practiced on the roofs of Brooklyn.[54]

According to Prof. Hessel of the Thünen Institute for Agricultural Technology in Braunschweig, the precision agriculture described here saves 5–10% in seed, fertilizer and pesticides.[55]

Finally, it should be stressed that multi-faceted "smart farming"must be seen in the wider context of societal trends. The increasingly established "farm to fork" strategy will contribute to the achievement of a largely digital circular economy. It will aim to reduce negative environmental impacts of food processing and retailing through AI processes in transportation, storage, packaging and food waste. Finally, the Farm to Fork strategy will stimulate sustainable food consumption and promote affordable healthy food for all.

---

[50] See Stefan Gröner/Stephanie Heinecke, op. cit. p. 174.

[51] See Thomas Hesse, Modern milking robot shows "Agriculture 4.0", in: RP.online of September 10, 2018.

[52] See Katharina Kropshofer, Von Schweinen und Maschinen Florian Bayer will künstliche Intelligenz in den Stall bringen, in: Der Standard, January 21, 2020.

[53] See Paul R. Daugherty/H. James Wilson, Human + Machine, Artificial Intelligence and the Future of Work, Munich, 2018, p. 46.

[54] https://netzfrauen.org/2016/05/02/new-york-eine-stadt-macht-satt-gemuese-von-den-daechern-brooklyns/

[55] Michael Latz, Can a field order itself a tractor?, in: NDR of 01.08.2019.

Fig. 4.4 Vertical agriculture (Source: Vincent Callebaut Architectures)

4.4   The Unemployed Reaper: K in Medicine

For the fifth of my annual check-ups, the door to the holy grail of radiology again opened for me only two hours after the agreed appointment. Asked about the delay, the attending physician replied that this could not be better planned because "every patient is different". My comment that the variance of customers—who, by the way, do not register—is significantly higher in supermarkets, where it is nevertheless possible to avoid queues, was scowlingly left uncommented.—It seems to me that the vision of my colleague Huss, according to which chatbot "Sophie" offers him a treatment appointment with parking space reservation to the minute, will have to wait a little longer for its realization.[56]

In contrast, AI can already demonstrate convincing successes in the field of medical diagnostics, from anamnesis to "theranostics".

Watson", for example, diagnosed the cause of a patient's symptoms as a rare form of leukaemia after only ten minutes by comparing millions of clinical pictures, something that

---

[56]Ralf Huss, op. cit. p. 2.

doctors had previously been unable to do for months.[57] Environmental engineers around Elena Naumova of the American University of Tufts have found out that the outbreak of epidemics can be predicted on the basis of the weather.[58] Already, wearable sensors, whether they be band-aids, wristwatches, necklaces or digital tattoos, are measuring and storing our most important medical data very accurately.[59] The smartphone thus becomes the "point of care".[60] High-tech patches use "nanosensors to measure blood glucose levels in the fluid around hair follicles on the skin and derive very reliable values for blood glucose levels."[61]

Especially in the diagnosis of breast and lung cancer, but also diabetic retinopathy, the AI "DeepMind" now achieves a better hit rate than human experts.[62] The AI also provides valuable support in the detection of blood cancer, especially acute myeloid leukaemia (AML). The approach is based on the analysis of the gene activity of cells found in the blood. At the German Center for Neurodegenerative Diseases (DZNE) in Bonn, under the direction of Prof. Joachim Schultze, thousands of genes are being investigated. The resulting "transcriptomes", the fingerprint of gene activity, so to speak, provide the relevant clues.[63] Christian Madl, head of the department of gastroenterology and hepatology at the Rudolfstiftung, notes that with a newly developed software docked to the endoscope, polyps are detected with 99.7% probability and several seconds faster than with the human eye during colonoscopy.[64] In this context, Dr. Altuna Akalin, head of the Bioinformatics Research Group at the Berlin Institute for Medical Systems Biology (BIMSB) of the Max Delbrück Center for Molecular Medicine (MDC), explains that with the "Multiomics Autoencoder Integration" ("maui") platform, one is able to "analyze multiple omics datasets and identify the most important patterns or features, in this case gene sets or indicators of colorectal cancer."[65]

The Hospital of the Brothers of Mercy in Regensburg also uses AI for colonoscopies in everyday clinical practice. According to Oliver Pech, head of the Department of Gastroenterology, the "artificial eye" detects more conspicuous changes in the mucous membrane than experts in colonoscopy.[66]

---

[57] Holger Volland, op. cit. p. 69.

[58] See Rotaviruses, weather report as infection forecast in: Süddeutsche Zeitung, 01.06.2012.

[59] See Jerry Kaplan, op. cit., p. 264 ff.

[60] See Jasper zu Putlitz, Die Zukunft der Versorgung chronisch kranker Menschen, in: Erwin Böttinger/, Jasper zu Putlitz (eds.), Die Zukunft der Medizin, Disruptive Innovationen revolutionieren Medizin und Gesundheit, Berlin, 2019, p. 25.

[61] Christian Maté, Medicine without Doctors, Salzburg/Vienna, 2020, p. 72.

[62] See Ibda, p. 6; Alexander Stindt, Breast cancer: Google AI diagnosis is more accurate than from radiologist, in: heilpraxis of 22.06.2020.

[63] See artificial intelligence detects blood cancer in: Medica Magazine, 09.01.2020.

[64] See artificial intelligence helps with colonoscopy in: Wien.ORF.at from 14.01.2020.

[65] See Deep learning detects molecular patterns of colorectal cancer in: MEDICA Magazine of 04.12.2019.

[66] See Bavarian hospital uses artificial intelligence for colonoscopy, in: Ärzteblatt of 21.01.2020.

In order to further improve colon cancer detection with AI, probiotics manufacturer Seed and software company Auggi are inviting people to take part in a somewhat unsavory but sensible participation campaign: Since every second person takes their smartphone to the toilet anyway, they're asking people to take a picture of the result and upload it directly to the company's website. The aim is to create a database "full of shit" to train an AI to analyze and classify human excreta.[67]

The Heidelberg University physicians have developed an AI software that accurately distinguishes black skin cancer from harmless moles.[68]

As already mentioned in Chap. 3, it was not until AI that it became clear that the chances of curing cancer not only depend on the nature of the cancer cells, but also to a large extent on the surrounding healthy cells.[69] At Tübingen University Hospital, a robot-based navigation system can be used to biopsy malignancy-specific areas of the prostate, which have previously been diagnosed using high-resolution examination technology.

Since more than 90% of cancer patients die not because of the primary tumor but because of the metastases, it is a significant medical advance if these can be located precisely and quickly. Georg Kofler writes: "Researchers led by Ali Ertürk at Helmholtz Zentrum München have now developed a method that can detect even the smallest metastases down to individual cancer cells in experimental mice. In a first step, the scientists make the mouse tissue transparent using a technique known as tissue clearing. Then they scan the entire body with a laser scanning microscope. The team has developed a novel deep-learning algorithm called DeepMACT. It can automatically detect and analyze cancer metastases and map the distribution of therapeutic antibodies. The algorithm detects metastases with comparable accuracy to a human expert—but at more than 300 times the speed, the researchers report."[70] The Watson Oncology Advisor also does telediagnosis for a hospital in Bangkok from Cornell University's Memorial Sloan Kettering Cancer Center in New York.[71]

The majority cause of death globally is not cancer but heart disease. A common cause is reduced blood flow. Medical researchers at University College London (UCL) have found that an AI is reliably able to predict the risk of heart attacks and strokes. By comparing blood flow results generated by the artificial intelligence with health outcomes, the researchers found that reduced blood flow increases the likelihood of heart attack, stroke or heart failure, and therefore the risk of premature death. The researchers used magnetic resonance tomographic scans of more than 1000 people and used a new automated artificial

---

[67] See Philip Pramer, House photos for science, in Der Standard, 19 Dec. 2019.

[68] See Walter Simon, op. cit. p. 12.

[69] See Ralf Huss, op. cit., p. 41 f.; Ulrike Till, Artificial intelligence in the fight against cancer in: SWR2, 04.02.2020.

[70] Georg Kofler, AI detects cancer metastases, in: Handelsblatt, 19.12.2020.

[71] See Ulrich Eberl, op. cit. p. 133.

intelligence technique to analyze these images. This made it possible to accurately and instantly quantify blood flow to the heart muscle.[72]

In Alzheimer's disease, deposits appear very early in the brain that are not visible to the bare eye. Special software, whose algorithm has been fed with more than 2000 brain scans, detects these deviations with 86% accuracy.[73] Using MRI scans of the brain, AI can predict whether babies would later develop autism. Thus, therapies can be applied early to mitigate the negative effects.[74]

Amazon's Alexa and IBM's Watson are said to be able to detect even colds and depression by voice pitch.[75] Based on the parents' ethnicity and income, an algorithm could even validly predict the obesity of their children.[76] Genomic goes one step further with the analysis of personal genetic data sets, which the US company "23 and Me" uses to offer health analyses of genetic diseases and predispositions. In 2013, the company was awarded a patent for a method that allows predictions of a desired child.[77]

In this context, the astonishing result of a Scandinavian research group is astounding and highly interesting. They found out by means of epigenetics that the grandchildren unconsciously still carry the war-related famine of their grandparents and thus gain weight more slowly than the corresponding control group.[78]

Prof. Stefan Lautenbacher and Prof. Miriam Kunz are trying to use new diagnostic algorithms for pain diagnostics. Since facial expressions are considered the best non-verbal pain indicator, the computer should learn to localize the face and its facial landmarks in the video image, extract features when the facial landmarks are displaced, and recognize pain based on these features.[79]

"Big Data" analyses are not unjustly accused of detecting mere correlations. Only causal links, however, reveal why a system behaves this way or that. "Anish Dhir and Ciarán Lee of UK digital health company Babylon Health want to change that using quantum cryptography: they have developed a method to identify causal relationships across different data sets. This could allow large databases of previously untapped medical data to be analysed for cause and effect—perhaps revealing newcausations."[80]

---

[72] See Alexander Stindt, How reliable is an AI for predicting stroke and heart attack? In: Heilpraxisnet.de from 16.02.2020.

[73] Philip Pramer, AI in medicine: when Alexa calls the rescue, in: Der Standard, 20.11.2019; see Ralf Huss, op. cit. p. 54.

[74] See Thomas Ramge, op. cit. p. 63.

[75] Ibid; see Holger Volland, op. cit. p. 109.

[76] Ibid.

[77] See Ralf Huss, op. cit. p. 36.

[78] See Ralf Huss, op. cit. p. 38.

[79] See Stefan Lautenbacher/Prof. Miriam Kunz, Kollege Computer hilft beim Schmerzmonitoring, in: Ärztezeitung vom 17.03.2020.

[80] Douglas Heaven, Quantum tricks for better computer medicine, in: heise online, 10.02.2020.

But AI is not only used in diagnosis. AI also opens up attractive opportunities in the development of new active substances.

"DSP-1181" is the name of a drug that has been brought to market in less than 12 months by Oxford-based biotech Exscientia and Japanese pharmaceutical company Sumitomo Dainippon Pharma. It was developed entirely by an artificial intelligence and is now being tested in clinical trials on the human body. The drug is a treatment for obsessive-compulsive disorder. The drug was created by algorithms that sifted through different compound possibilities based on a huge database of parameters.[81]

Bayer AG, for example, is increasingly relying on artificial intelligence in its research into active substances to combat heart disease and cancer, and has therefore entered into a cooperation with Exscientia, a British specialist in active substance research and molecule design.[82] This is where "Big Data" comes into play again. The pharmaceutical company Novartis has established the Data42 project to use the treasure trove of data from several decades of research on the best-selling psoriasis drug Cosentyx to derive an extension of indications or to search for new active ingredients.[83]

Analogous to personalised products, as described in Chap. 5, the trend towards personalised active ingredients (precision medicine) is also being attempted in pharmaceutics.[84] ETH Professor Schneider warns, however, that the right biomarkers must first be found for "drug design" with algorithms.[85] This is the task of computational biology, which collects all the information available from patients.[86]

The Watson Discovery Advisor with its huge database is also used in the search for new drugs.[87]

However, the successes of AI-supported therapy approaches are also clearly visible. The start-up "Nia Health", for example, has developed an app to make life easier for neurodermatitis sufferers. To do this, patient data are analyzed using artificial intelligence, with the machine-vision algorithm examining images of inflamed skin areas to make recommendations to doctors and patients.[88] The app "Woebot" is said to show success

---

[81] See Drug developed entirely by AI is used for the first time in: t3n from 03.02.2020.

[82] See Michel Doepke, Bayer focuses on artificial intelligence—is the stock a buy now? In: Der Aktionär, 10.01.2020.

[83] See Holger Alich, Where Novartis relies on artificial intelligence, in Berliner Zeitung, December 10, 2019.

[84] See Ralf Huss, op. cit. p. 5 and p. 57.

[85] See Holger Alich, Where Novartis relies on artificial intelligence, in Berliner Zeitung, December 10, 2019.

[86] See Ralf Huss, op. cit. p. 32.

[87] See Ulrich Eberl, op. cit., p. 134; Andre Borbe, IBM launches Watson Discovery Advisor in the cloud, in: Silicon.de, 28.08.2014.

[88] Jürgen Stüber, Diese App will Menschen mit Neurodermitis helfen, in: Gründerszene vom February 14, 2020.

against depression after just 2 weeks of use.[89] Alexa, which we already know, uses an app to help diabetics manage their condition.[90] The description of medical apps could be continued at will. Not all of them seem useful. Instead of using the app to locate the closest defibrillator, it's probably smarter to call the emercency service right away. The same will probably also apply to the emergency software "SmED" (= Structured Initial Medical Assessment Procedure for Germany) of the National Association of panel doctors.[91]

The so-called nanorobots (= "nanites") have a much more practical significance in the field of biomedicine:

- With the chemosensor, glucose monitoring is successfully carried out to diagnose and treat diabetes. Glucose molecules in the bloodstream precisely determine the necessary amount of insulin to be injected.
- Dentifrobots cause desensitization of the teeth and oral analgesia.
- Nanorobots bring the drug precisely to the target point in the body
- Nanorobots can use the polymer transferrin to recognize and kill tumor cells without harming the healthy cells.
- Genetic diseases can be treated by nanorobots by interfering with the molecular structure of the DNA in the defective cells.

These nanites can also be used in the treatment of cerebral aneurysms (protrusion in the wall of a blood vessel in the brain) and in the removal of kidney stones. Such nanosystems can contain magnetic materials, so that these systems can be detected and also controlled from outside with magnetic fields in the human body.[92]

Remote-controlled robots now make surgeons "cut safe" by "calculating away" the trembling of his hand.[93] The MiroSurge system of the German Aerospace Center is also a tremor-free and precise robotic aid for robot-assisted surgery on the beating heart.[94] In the future, mixed and augmented reality applications will even largely eliminate the spatial separation of the screen and the surgical area.[95]

Nanorobots can also already act as semi-autonomous surgeons on site in the human body these days. For example, a micropipette that vibrates rapidly at a frequency of 100 Hz with a tip diameter of less than 1 μm can be used to cut dendrites from individual neurons. In doing so, it is programmed and guided by human surgeons. The robotic phlebotomist

---

[89] Andrea Cornelius, op. cit. p. 69.

[90] Ralf Otte, op. cit., p. 91.

[91] See Ralf Huss, op. cit. p. 66.

[92] See Simone Schürle-Finke, Nanosystems for Personalised Medicine, in: Erwin Böttinger/Jasper zu Putlitz (eds.), op. cit., p. 96 f.

[93] Manuela Lenzen, op. cit., p. 154 f.

[94] See https://www.dlr.de/rm/mirosurge#gallery/28728

[95] See Igor Maximilian Sauer et al., Operating in Digital Space—Mixed Reality in Surgery, in: Erwin Böttinger/Jasper zu Putlitz (eds.), op. cit. p. 73.

Veebot autonomously performs blood sampling. For this purpose, the fixed arm is scanned with an infrared camera in order to locate the most suitable vein. Only when ultrasound has verified that the vein found is large enough and contains sufficient blood does the robot insert the needle.[96]

Research leaders Stéphanie Lacour and Grégoire Courtine, together with their team from the Swiss Federal Institute of Technology Lausanne (EPFL), Switzerland, have developed an implant that enables paraplegic rats to regain the ability to walk through a combination of electrical and chemical stimulation and subsequent movement training. The special feature is the flexibility and softness of the material, which can release electrical impulses and pharmacological substances simultaneously.[97]

In the meantime, people like to talk about "robo-doctors". However, this is a term that gives the wrong impression. The term "medical robot" is probably more appropriate to make it clear that the human doctor is still the sovereign in the operating room.

The company "Intuitive Surgical" has already created a possibility of minimally invasive, robot-assisted surgery for the urological and gynaecological field for years with the operating system "Da Vinci". The current competitor is called "Miro" from the Institute of Robotics and Mechatronics of the German Aerospace Center (DLR), which offers similar functionality to Da Vince. Miro can be programmed to avoid putting certain areas of the body at risk. The robot controls the doctor's hand and stops a slip if necessary. Using remote control with force feedback, the doctor senses how much force he is applying and where there is resistance, as if he were palpating the patient with his finger. The "Renaissance" system from Mazor Robotics is only the size of a hand. Its robotic arm, including surgical instruments, fixes itself precisely to a pre-programmed position so that the doctor can operate with precision.

Still nameless is the "agile thin", a "continuum robot", which with its 1–2 mm small, tentacle-like arms made of several superelastic tubes can open up spaces that are difficult to access in a minimally invasive way, for example to perform a brain tumour operation through the nose (see Fig. 4.5). Minimally invasive surgery is therefore already well established. But in the meantime quantum physicists like Michio Kaku can already imagine non-invasive medicine. Ray Kurzweil takes a very concrete position on this and predicts non-invasive surgery for the 2030s.[98]

Another medical application of AI is implants and exoskeletons. The "cochlear" implant, for example, is an electronic medical device that takes over the function of the damaged parts of the inner ear (the cochlea) to transmit audio signals to the brain. With the introduction of microsurgical techniques and 3D printing, the reconstruction of larger bony

---

[96] See Tekla S. Perry, Profile: Veebot, Making a robot that can draw blood faster and more safely than a human can, in: IEEE Spectrum, July 26, 2013.

[97] See Tanja Konrad, Stretchable neuroimplant for the treatment of spinal cord injuries, in: Der Querschnitt.de of January 09, 2017.

[98] Ray Kurzweil, op. cit. p. 244.

Fig. 4.5 The "agile skinny"
(Source: SciencePhotoLibrary)

defects in maxillofacial surgery has also become a successful procedure that allows implants to be fitted with millimeter precision.[99] The Californian company Align Technology produces transparent dental splints in Ciudad Juárez, Mexico. With the aid of a special computer graphics process, starting from the actual state of the dentition, which is recorded in jaw models with a patient identification number, a previously determined treatment goal is represented three-dimensionally and divided into individual treatment phases. For each of these phases, individual splints are then produced, each of which is worn for approximately 2 weeks. During this time, the teeth are continuously moved in the previously calculated direction by applying pressure. Then the next splint follows until the desired treatment goal is reached. Depending on the degree of malocclusion, the treatment usually lasts between about 6 and about 18 months.

Who would have ever expected that competitive athletes would once resist facing disabled people in competition? Medical technology makes it possible for leg amputees to have a good chance of winning the race. More important, however, is the benefit of AI to everyday medical practice. Trained digital watches not only detect signs of Parkinson's disease very early on via their sensors, they also treat it by compensating for the contractions in the patient's arm muscles by vibrating.[100]

Exoskeleton suits enable paralyzed people to walk again. The Hybrid Assistive Limb, or HAL, is a servo exoskeleton suit developed by Tsukuba University in Japan and robotics company Cyberdyne Inc. Nerve signals are sent from the brain to the muscles via movement neurons, which cause the musculoskeletal system to move. This creates low-threshold biosignals at the skin surface that can be detected and derived. The HAL robotic suit registers these signals through a sensor on the wearer's skin and transmits them to its servo unit, which moves the particular joint to be supported. AI also makes it possible

---

[99] See Alexander Kübler, Modern forms of therapy of oral cavity carcinoma, lecture of January 26, 2020.

[100] See Ilka Koplin, Mit Künstlicher Intelligenz gegen Parkinson, in: FAZ, 11.08.2019; Stephanie Zweig, op. cit. p. 102.

with neural control of prosthetics to connect humans and machines in such a way that limbs can be replaced with them. The best-known success of this methodology is probably the "Walk Again Project", in which a paraplegic was allowed to kick the first ball at the 2014 Soccer World Cup.[101]

AI-assisted brainwaves help paraplegics to control wheelchairs, and brain-computer interfaces enable direct information transfer between an organic brain and a technical circuit, making it possible, for example, to control a cursor, operate a virtual spelling program or control robotic or prosthetic effectors.[102] Professor Courtine of the Swiss Federal Institute of Technology in Lausanne (EPFL) is reteaching paraplegics how to walk using an "electronic bridge" that transmits signals from the brain to the motor nerves of the lower spinal cord.[103] Swedish truck driver Magnus Niska has a bionic arm implanted directly into his skeleton. His nerves are linked to sensors in his arm so he can feel and grasp things, allowing him to do his job.[104] Researchers at Harvard University are working on a soft robot that wraps around the heart like a hand and can assist it when needed, like a pacemaker.[105]

Finally, a word about cryonics. Whether the revival of cryopreserved people will really work one day is completely uncertain. But at least more than 400 people have already been frozen into "cryosleep".[106]

It will be interesting to see what AI—in conjunction with synthetic biology, for example—has in store for medicine in the future. It can already be said that it has so far proved to be a field of application with above-average dynamics. This really cannot be said for the teaching area that will be dealt with next.

4.5   IQ for Everyone: AI in Education

If you took a wheelwright of the nineteenth century to the glass VW factory near Dresden, where the modern "wagon makers" work, the poor man wouldn't know in the least what was happening around him, even though it was his successor profession. A housewife from the same period would not even be able to boil water in a modern kitchen with induction stove and coffee machine, let alone prepare a dish there.—If, on the other hand, one were to invite Adalbert Stifter to visit a school, he might wonder about the many drinking bottles, about the cozy corner, or about the coffeehouse seating, but he wouldn't need to look for

---

[101] See The World Cup has begun!, in: RP. online of June 12, 2014.

[102] See Erik Brynjolfsson/Andrew Mcafee, op. cit. p. 114 f.

[103] See He teaches paraplegics to walk, in: Welt from February 27, 2020.

[104] See Holger Volland, op. cit. p. 173.

[105] See Manuela Lenzen, op. cit. p. 105.

[106] See Why we can't freeze humans and wake them up in a hundred years, in: Quarks, August 1, 2019.

the chalk or the blackboard sponge! While all areas of our lives have changed dramatically in the last hundred years, education has remained technically unaffected. Whether this is due to the general permanency of education providers remains to be seen.

When the former grammar school teacher and Minister President of Baden-Württemberg, Kretschmann, recently announced that spelling no longer needed to be learned, as there was now appropriate software for this, he reaped a mighty "shit-storm". But isn't he right? We don't learn anymore to carve poisoned arrows to kill mammoths or to splice quills to be able to write. And today's young people don't know what to do with a slide rule either, since there are now calculators for logarithmic and trigonometric functions. But our humanistic educated elites still recommend Latin as the first foreign language, even if nobody speaks it anymore except for a few clerics. The author himself managed the great Latinum with good success and great affection, and yet today he rates it as a "detour production" and would have preferred to learn Spanish straight away, in order to be able to make himself understood by millions of people. Especially since Caesar's "De bello Gallico" could not particularly shape him humanistically.

The author had to experience first-hand the aversion that educational institutions have towards new media: In 1987, he gave Germany's first virtual lecture from the video studio at the University of Applied Sciences Würzburg-Schweinfurt, which was worth a report by the German public broadcaster. When the author reported on it at the following didactics conference of the Bavarian Ministry of Culture, he only received a displeasing shake of the head from the responsible ministerial councilor. The colleague lecturing afterwards began her media-less presentation with the derisive words: "I am still the medium myself!" and received a benevolent nod of the head from the aforementioned ministry official and enthusiastic applause from the audience. And even today, at most of the lectures of the "Virtual University of Bavaria", one has the impression that VR and AR have not yet been invented.

Enough of the gloating—now let the few AI applications in education be showcased.

Professor of Applied Computer Science Ute Schmid expects the combination of intelligent systems and human competence to bring "good added value" to education. She herself has developed an intelligent tutor system that produces individual diagnoses in written subtraction and could also be used in language teaching. She also has an AI-driven module ready for vocational training that has learned to classify facial expressions with relative reliability. This could be used to train nurses to recognise that patients are not looking angry but are in pain when they contract their eyes and simultaneously tighten their mouths.[107] Basically, however, it should be noted that only a minority of 2.7% of companies use AI in corporate training.[108]

---

[107] See interview with Ute Schmid on Deutschlandfunk on June 27, 2019.

[108] See Ute Wolter, Bestandsaufnahme: KI in der betrieblichen Bildung, in: Personalwirtschaft of September 26, 2019.

Microsoft offers the "School of **Tomorrow**" a plastic reader with which students can record and play back a text that they themselves have read aloud. They can also display syllables while reading—gosh! "That's awesome," I can already hear the "digital natives" yelling. They go on to say, "Using facial recognition and eye trackers, AI can detect if a child is having difficulty reading at a certain point and offer them assistance at that exact moment. For example, reading assistance is turned on or an explanation window opens."[109] This compares to the textbooks being developed in the learning lab at the German Research Center for Artificial Intelligence in Kaiserslautern, which use facial recognition to check whether children can follow what they are reading. If children's eyes linger too long on a piece of text, additional information is played.[110] In the USA, there are already math classes where the AI computer works out daily timetables depending on the students' performance level. The solutions are recorded on the tablet and either the same tasks are presented again or a more difficult task level is offered.[111] Alexander Siebert, founder and CEO of Retresco, promises the following as an AI application: "Individualised learning profiles highlight the respective strengths, weaknesses and progress of the learners and help to recognise these. To address these learning needs, the AI itself compiles individualized tasks and materials based on the learning profile. Learners can thus work on topics based on their strengths."[112]

Scientists at the German Research Center for Artificial Intelligence (DFKI) have initiated the "Hypermind" project together with the Technical University of Kaiserslautern. The "intelligent textbook" developed there, which can recognize and analyze the direction of the reader's gaze, is intended to support students individually and to systematically document their learning success. Both static and dynamic multimedia representations—such as sounds, superimposed images or film sequences—are intended to enrich the individual processing of the textbook content. The future smart school will also include digital boards and data glasses and the use of textbooks in which a hypertextual layer is added to a real image.

For learning a foreign language in the pre-school sector, the European Commission funded the project "2TOR" (= Tutor), in which the child-friendly language robot "Robin" not only communicates verbally, but also takes gestures and other body language into account.

A study has just been published showing that a machine-learning system that uses artificial intelligence to respond to each patient's idiosyncrasies has been successfully used

---

[109] https://cloudblogs.microsoft.com/industry-blog/de-de/education/2019/12/05/ki-in-lehre-und-unterricht/

[110] See Verena Gonsch, Chancen und Risiken von KI im Klassenzimmer, in: https://www.netzwerk-digitale-bildung.de/blog/chancen-und-risiken-von-ki-im-klassenzimmer

[111] Ibid.

[112] Alexander Siebert, Artificial Intelligence in Education? How Teachers and Technology Complement Each Other, in: Science Year 2919, November 25, 2019; https://www.physik.uni-kl.de/kuhn/forschung/aktuelle-projekte/

with autistic schoolchildren. Participants were asked to solve math problems on a touchscreen tablet. Using a reinforcement learning algorithm, the game was personalized. While the focus of the game was math, its inauthentic purpose was to teach the children social skills.[113]

At least it can be stated that the sector of "Educational Technologies" (EdTech) is growing, but the practical use in German schools is still proving to be very hesitant. Felix Müller says: "The role of the teacher is only changing, away from knowledge replicator to learning coach, who simply accompanies the students in this process. In that respect, Germany is now a candidate, especially in the education sector, which tends to stick to the old."

For higher education, the German Federal Ministry of Education and Research (BMBF) has allocated funding for a hundred new AI professorships in 2019. So far, however, the British computer scientist and neuroscientist Peter Dayan is the only new AI professor that the German government can present.[114] So there is still "room for improvement".

4.6   Why Do We Still Need Dexterous Hands: AI in Business and Technology?

Separate chapters are dedicated to the economic fields of trade and Industry 4.0. Other application examples are documented here.

3D printing began in 2010 with the ability to print out plastic figurines for home use. After model making quickly took up this new technology, it has now reached the factory floor as "additive manufacturing". In addition to the printer, no further tools are needed to create workpieces, and additional processing times such as machining or milling are no longer necessary. The 3D printer also makes it possible to produce objects with complex geometries that are very difficult or impossible to manufacture using conventional production methods. Its application is even more diverse since not only plastics but also metallic and ceramic materials can be processed. In the meantime, architects are not only designing their models using 3D printing, but the construction industry is already using it to build houses. With the help of a mobile 3D printer, the US company Apis Cor, for example, has constructed a two-storey building for the Dubai Municipality.[115]

There are no practical applications to report yet. But 4D printing is already in the research field's sights. It is a 3D printing process that brings a fourth dimension, time, into play. This allows objects to move and/or change under a certain sensory trigger, such as

---

[113] See Sascha Mattke, AI help for autistic children: machine learning system as individual therapist, in. Heise online, February 28, 2020.

[114] See https://www.bmbf.de/de/kuenstliche-intelligenz-5965.html; Katharina Menne, Gesucht: 100 Superhirne, in: Die Zeit, February 20, 2020.

[115] Denny Gille, This is how the world's largest 3D printed house was created, in: handwerk.com from February 26, 2020.

contact with water, heat, vibration or sound (intelligent material) and, for example, garden furniture to adapt to an uneven lawn.

The construction industry has already been mentioned above. In this context, it is worth noting that the construction robot Hadrian from the Australian company Fastbrick Robotics completed an entire house with 0.5 mm precision in just two days. Hadrian reads the 3D construction plans, grabs the bricks with its 28-m-long gripper arm, spreads mortar over them and stoically places brick after brick without tiring.[116]

The construction sector is more digital than one would expect anyway: The surveying drone from Kassel-based specialist drone provider AiBotix surveyed a large construction site covering 16 ha in a fully automated flight within eight minutes. In its pre-programmed flight, the drone surveys much more precisely than humans can with levelling devices and measuring rods.

Building Information Modeling (BIM) is also an AI-supported method for the networked planning, execution and management of buildings and other structures. All relevant building data is digitally modelled, combined and recorded. The building is also geometrically visualized as a virtual model. Building Information Modeling is used both in the construction industry and in facility management.

Exoskeletons can enhance the performance of construction workers during heavy work, transforming them into "construction cyborgs." Robots can scan interior spaces, query operating conditions using sensors embedded in the building, and provide case-specific documentation to ensure that requested maintenance is completed quickly and flawlessly. The British company Q-Bot offers robots that crawl under floors to apply thermal insulation.[117]

The symbiosis of AI and nature is also interesting when you look at biomimetic robots. Here, the Esslingen-based company Festo in particular has a lot to show. "In the artificial kangaroo, Festo intelligently combines pneumatic and electric drive technology to create a highly dynamic system. Stability during jumping and landing is ensured by the stable jump kinematics and the precise control and regulation technology. The consistent lightweight design promotes the unique jumping behaviour. The system is controlled by gestures. Like its natural model, it can recover the energy when jumping, store it and efficiently reintroduce it in the next jump."[118] The Smart Bird can take off, fly and land on its own without additional propulsion. With an active articulated torsion drive, the wings can not only flap up and down, but also purposefully twist to simulate real bird flight. Similar qualities are demonstrated by the BionikOpter, which technically implements the highly complex flight characteristics of the dragonfly.

Air Jelly is a bionics project that was also developed as part of Festo's Bionic Learning Network. The "flying jellyfish" consists of a ballonet filled with helium. Air Jelly is the first

---

[116] See Australian robot Hadrian walls up house in 48 hours, in: Ingenieur.de from July 1, 2015.

[117] See Ulrich Eberl, op. cit. p. 181 f.

[118] https://www.festo.com/group/de/cms/10219.htm

indoor flying object with peristaltic propulsion (muscle activity of hollow organs). In addition, there is the Aquajelly for underwater use, which also works according to the "Fin-Ray-Effect".

Bionics also served as the basis for the innovation in the FlexShapeGripper from Festo. Just as the chameleon catches insects by placing its tongue over its prey, the FlexShapeGripper uses this technology to grip a wide variety of objects with a positive fit. With its elastic silicone cap, it can even pick up and collect several objects in one gripping process. The bionic gripper consists of a double-acting cylinder, one chamber of which is filled with compressed air, while the second is permanently filled with water. The elastic silicone moulded part, which corresponds to the tongue of the chameleon, is mounted on it. During the gripping process, the gripper is guided over the object so that it touches the object with its silicone cap. Then the upper pressure chamber is vented and the water-filled silicone part pulls inward. At the same time, the gripper is pulled further over the object. The silicone cap then slips over any gripping object of any shape, creating a tight form-fit. The elastic silicone allows precise adaptation to a wide range of geometries.[119]

The aim of the BMBF-funded research project "BioLas.exe" of the Institute of Biology II at RWTH Aachen University in the field of Cellular Neurobionics and the Fraunhofer Institute for Production Technology IPT, which has been running since 2012, is to transfer the structures of the lizard skin to technical components and thus improve wetting with lubricants and other fluids. The bionic surfaces modeled on the lizard skin could be used on bearings, shafts or sealing rings, for example, to better distribute fluids such as oils, lubricants or coolants and to reduce the wear of pumps and motors. However, to date, no results seem to have been achieved for practical use.[120]

To conclude the bionics examples, the "fin-ray effect" should be mentioned once again. With the patented "fin-ray effect", Festo AG designed the Airacuda, which imitates the drive of the fin fish. The technical fish is modelled on real fish in terms of function, construction and shape. The tail fin of the Air-Ray has a fluid muscle which alternately shortens the diagonals in the structure, resulting in the back and forth movement of the tail fin. With a color sensor, the Air-Ray sorts color balls above water and the Aqua-Ray sorts color balls under water (see Fig. 4.6).

It will be interesting to see what other miraculous products the combination of so-called nanomuscles and AI will bring to light. After all, the artificial muscles and corresponding sensors at the Georgia Institute of Technology in Atlanta have created a staircase with a spring mechanism that reduces the effort required to climb stairs by 20% and the strain on the knees by 38%.[121]

---

[119] See https://www.festo.com/group/de/cms/10217.htm

[120] See Dorothee Quitter, Bionic surfaces for technical components, in: Vogel Verlag Konstruktionspraxis from October 31, 2012.

[121] See Jan Oliver Löfken, Staircase with spring mechanism, in: Welt der Physik, July 12, 2017.

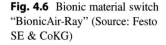

Fig. 4.6 Bionic material switch "BionicAir-Ray" (Source: Festo SE & CoKG)

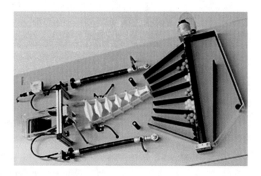

The author has been in the field of HR diagnostics for a long time and finds it hard to see AI replacing his expertise. But there is no denying that software packages are coming onto the market under the title of "Recruitment Smart Technologies" that successfully "dehumanise" the recruitment process and optimise it in the process. London-based Sniper AI, for example, is an artificial intelligence for the recruitment process that matches résumés and job descriptions with remarkable speed and stunning accuracy, filtering out the best match without prejudice. Berlin-based Viasto offers an interview generator with specific interview guides for each position requirement in the video interview. While it still assures that AI only complements the hiring process, it does not replace the recruiter. But one can expect that the algorithms will be further developed in order to be able to satisfactorily assess not only the professional competence, but also the social characteristics of the applicants. This is all the more important as the hiring decisions made using the conventional method to date are not error-free.[122]

Another field of AI is virtual reality (VR) and augmented reality (AR). In the latter, reality is augmented, for example by an artificial bar in ski flying or in football to mark the offside line. With VR, nothing is real anymore, it is exclusively computer-generated "reality". With the augmented reality "glasses" from Google Glass or Sony SmartEyeglass you can, among other things, look at the Internet and social media or, for example, look at holograms of your own four walls, whereby Google Glass is not a pair of glasses but a small computer mounted on the glasses and with the SmartEye from Sony a display is projected onto the lenses and a camera is attached to the glasses, while the control unit works externally (e.g. mobile phone) via a cable connection. Incidentally, the new version "Google Glass Enterprise" is intended for business use, similar to "Hololens" from Mircosoft. Today, VR is mainly used in the film and media industry to realize "impossible" worlds. But industry is also using it. For example, "Lightshape" is used to create walk-through virtual 3D environments of cars, which can be used to better evaluate the design of new models.[123] Possible future applications of VR are described in Chap. 8.

---

[122] See Nadine Bös, Auswahl von Bewerbern—Mitarbeiter nach Bauchgefühl, in: FAZ of December 12, 2019.

[123] See Angela Frank, KI und VR: Neue Chancen für Kreativschaffende, in: MFG Baden -Württemberg of August 1, 2019.

Of the many AI-based products with artful features, the OrCam is presented here as an example. The wireless OrCam MyReader 2 is a pair of data glasses that reads texts from any media to blind or visually impaired people by picking up the texts with a mini-camera and relaying them to the ear of the person wearing the glasses via the built-in speaker. Not only that—the Orcam also recognizes faces, products, bills, and colors, and is as inexpensive as ordinary hearing aids.

Finally, we should mention walking robots, which have been used commercially for a long time. The model list is long and ranges from cat-, dog-, horse- and insect-like species to numerous human-like forms. Altlas, the "forest man" has already been mentioned. Cassie, from Agility Robotics, is a headless biped that can act as a delivery robot, like a human messenger, bringing pizza or groceries up stairs to even one of the upper floors.[124] Against Cassie, Handle, the latest 2017 creation from Boston Dynamics is a giant 2 m tall that can lift up to 45 kg, jump 1.20 m high and run 25 km. It is best used for loading and unloading. In contrast, the six-wheeled parcel robot from the logistics company Hermes is tiny, but a promising delivery alternative in urban areas.[125]

As is often the case, many of the AI solutions presented here were originally developed for the military sector. And probably even more amazing and advanced innovations could be found there. But the author explicitly excludes the military sector in his reflections on AI for many reasons.

---

[124] See Werner Pluta, Delivery robot Cassie can walk and climb stairs, in: golem.de from May 3, 2018.

[125] See Florentin Schumacher, Achtung, Rollpost, in: Spiegel, October 5, 2016.

Are You Still Buying or Are You Already "Influencing"?: Trade 4.0

5

> *For a man to act, his own self is a poor starting point.*
> *Francis Bacon*

Let's get this straight right away: Influencers have nothing to do with AI. Even natural intelligence would not come to mind first when you look at the blogs. And this statement can probably also be extended to the followers. But AI becomes relevant again when the platforms on which the "influence" takes place push the influencer fumes together into mountains of data in order to subject them to "predictive analytics" with algorithms.

5.1 Without Advertising, the Marketing Mix Is "Nix" (Nothing): AI in Marketing

Especially in modern marketing, AI is becoming increasingly important and is causing dramatic changes in retail. Henry Ford's complaint that half of advertising expenditure is money wasted, but unfortunately we don't know which half, is no longer justified in times of Big Data and personalised advertising messages. In the case of digital advertising, the interdependence between advertising campaign and sales can be measured quite precisely.[1]

However, before you get to the tailored approach to the individual customer, there is a lot of AI-based market research to be done first. The techniques of digital pattern recognition, which Nassehi calls the "third discovery of society",[2] not only make market

---

[1] See Andreas Wagener, op. cit. p. 63.

[2] See Armin Nassehi, Patterns, Theory of Digital Society, 2nd ed, Munich, 2019, p. 59.

© Springer Fachmedien Wiesbaden GmbH, part of Springer Nature 2021
G. Cisek, *The Triumph of Artificial Intelligence*,
https://doi.org/10.1007/978-3-658-34896-0_5

segmentation more precise, they also often bring to light surprising correlations. For example, the British hotel chain Jurys discovered a correlation between media use and booking behaviour in that many customers were looking for hotels near football stadiums. Accordingly, the chain configured a specific offer for this target group and was thus able to increase bookings significantly.[3]

Big Data analyses sort the market into clusters, not social but valid statistical groups with collective market behaviour, in order to infer selective marketing measures.[4]

Here, of course, the large platforms have a considerable advantage over other market participants, as they can build up data monopolies with their "mining rights".[5] There is already talk of "platform capitalism", in which the intermediaries GAFA (Google, Apple, Facebook, Amazon) and BAT (Baidu, Alibaba, Tencent) not only dominate the market, but also control customer behaviour.[6] Or as French philosopher Michel Foucoult put it, "The citizen is free to do what he wants, but should want what he should."[7] It is not without reason that Facebook has bought the software manufacturer Wit-ai or the companies PredictionIO and MetaMind, which specialise in forecasting, in order to be able to use them to extract the huge treasures of data in a qualified manner. Cluster analyses are used to compile target groups and their behavioral characteristics in order to derive cluster-specific marketing measures.

This brings us to AI-guided targeting, where a distinction is usually made between:

- **Environment and sociodemographic targeting**
  (Placement of online advertising on suitable website environments)
- **Regional targeting/geo-targeting**
  (according to the origin of the customers)
- **Keyword targeting**
  (Online advertising based on search engine queries or business search engines)
- **Context targeting**
  (online advertising based on initiated clicks of relevant environments)
- **Technical targeting**
  (Online advertising depending on the technical equipment of the customer)
- **CRM targeting**
  (Placement of advertising material and information with regard to already existing customer data)
- **Behavioural targeting**

---

[3] See Andreas Wagener, op. cit. p. 132.

[4] See Armin Nassehi, op. cit. 2019, p. 302.

[5] See Christoph Keese, Silicon Germany, Wie wir die digitale Transformation schaffen, 1st edition, Munich, 2016, p. 99.

[6] See https://de.wikipedia.org/wiki/Plattformkapitalismus

[7] Quoted from Armin Nassehi, op. cit. p. 307.

(based on the analysis of the surfing behaviour (click paths) of an Internet user)
- **Predictive behavioral targeting**
  (based on information from the surfing behaviour of users with information from other data sources such as survey or registration data)
- **Semantic targeting**
  (not by keywords, but by total visible texts and main topics, for which topic-specific online campaigns are placed).[8]

Statistical bots are already being used to automatically uncover meaningful data relationships. Within the defined target groups, opinions and sentiments about products can be siphoned off by means of opinion mining and sentiment mining.

Let's now move on to the advertising measures that are based on AI. With search engine marketing (SEM) as a subarea of online marketing, measures are taken to attract visitors to a website via web search engines. A distinction is made between search engine advertising (SEA) and search engine optimization (SEO).

SEA is used to place ads on search engine results pages. Usually, these are ads in text form that promote offers that match the user's search query.

SEO refers to measures that serve to increase the visibility of a website and its content for users of a web search engine. Optimization refers to the improvement of unpaid results in organic search engine rankings (natural listings) and excludes direct traffic and the purchase of paid advertising. Unlike organic search results with SEO, in SEA, advertisements are financed through auction processes and their ranking depends on, among other things, the relevance of the web page linked in the search ad to the search term and the amount of the bid (Paid Listing). The latest trend in this regard is called "Smart Bidding" at Google. Here, the ad customer can choose between different strategies: If he does not decide between CPA (Cost Per Action), ROAS (Return On Advertising Spend) or CPC (Cost Per Click), he can also choose the category "Maximize Conversions" in general.

In addition to advertising products, search engine marketing is increasingly used for corporate branding and public relations.

Real-time advertising (RTA) should also be mentioned in this context. RTA, also referred to as "Programmatic Advertising", includes both the individual playout of banners per individual ad impression (= call-up of advertising media) and the bidding process, namely the individual bids per ad impression. RTA focuses on the individual user. For each individual ad impression offered, an associated user profile is supplied so that the advertiser can decide whether he wants to bid precisely on this user profile.

Another form of "digital marketing"(Offline channels such as TV, SMS etc. are also used in addition to online marketing) is content marketing. It focuses on creating and distributing valuable, relevant and consistent content to attract defined target groups and ultimately generate profitable customer action. Influencer marketing also falls into this category, but it has little to do with AI, as it's more about digital word-of-mouth advertising

---

[8] See Andreas Wagener, op. cit. p. 109.

for followers. It's different with content marketing automation. Here, using an AI content generator and NLP methods—usually based on keywords—existing content on the web is sifted and automatically processed into new content targeted at relevant customer groups in the company's own product range. This is why we also speak of "content curation".

Let's move on from target group-oriented marketing to personalized Customer Relation Management (CRM). If, once again, when you're Googling, you get the message: "Customers who bought ... also bought ...", then a so-called recommendation engine was obviously at work. It first quantified your interest in the product you clicked on and then recommended alternatives or additional products to you on this basis, so that you save yourself the trouble of further searching. The Common Wealth Bank of Australia (CBA) won the "Model Bank Winner" award for its "Customer Engagement Engine". The CBA program focuses on "customer journeys" analyzed at scale. Every customer approach—whether online, mobile, in the call center, at the ATM or in the branch—triggers a call in CEE (Customer Electronics Edition), which makes a recommendation for the "next best conversation" in 150–300 ms.

AI also takes in all the touchpoints on your customer journey, then uses NLP to send you personalized emails. With Google Assistant, it doesn't stop at emails. It permanently accompanies the user by whispering real-time weather and traffic data or even financial and sports information, recommending cinema tips and structuring travel plans. It even imitates the writing style and tone of the person being courted.

The numerous platform chatbots such as Siri, Cortana, etc., which are able to conduct individual customer conversations, have already been mentioned earlier. For example, "Clara" at the mail order company Otto is not just a multi-purpose cabinet or dining room chair, but also a chatbot with the same name that answers questions about service and orders.[9]

A special recommendation software is found for the music industry. "How much music recommendation does a person need?" asks HORST (Holistic Recommendation and StoryTelling Technology). HORST is a demonstrator for "Holistic/Hybrid Recommendation and Explanation" developed by the DFKI (Deutsches Forschungszentrum für Künstliche Intelligenz). As a user, you click on your "desired musical nuts" and then get recommendations that are backed up with interesting facts and stories.

Similar to content marketing, in which advisory and entertaining content is intended to appeal to the target group, AI makes so-called "native advertising" (advertising in a familiar environment) possible. The content is designed by content bots in such a way that it is hardly recognizable as advertising, but appears like editorial contributions. With content augmentation, existing content is supplemented and "spruced up" to increase engagement rates.[10] Companies like Phrasee for voice texts or Yala especially for videos

---

[9] See Peter Gentsch, op. cit. p. 59.

[10] See Andreas Wagener, op. cit. p. 98 f.; Peter Gensch, op. cit. p. 44.

offer services for this. Facebook compiles customer audiences for which ads are placed on Facebook, Instagram and the Audience Network.

There is now also an international provider market for the sale of "digital advertising inventory", where publishers and marketers offer their advertising space and advertising media on their websites or apps for advertising bookings. In order to measure the advertising success and assess the efficiency of the individual advertising media and media channels, the AdServer logs the ad impressions, i.e. the clicks, leads, sales and orders, which can then be used to determine the conversion ratios.

The results should be used to improve customer experience management (CEM or CXM). Satisfied customers should become loyal customers and loyal customers should become "enthusiastic ambassadors" ("brand as a friend") of the brand or product ("satisfied—loyal—advocate"). In this context, it has already been shown that the offers must not only be customer-specific, but must also be concise in the face of an increasingly shrinking attention limit (attention economy).[11]

With the Alexa Skill Kit (ASK) from Amazon's Echo family, providers can build new custom capabilities. The ASK is a collection of APIs and tools with which advertising messages can be transported highly selectively in the sense of "conversational assisted commerce" to smart speakers, smart TVs, cars, etc.

Today, modern retail companies decide on customer expenditure and measures according to the customer lifetime value (CLV), i.e. the contribution margin that a customer realizes during his entire "customer life", discounted to the point in time under consideration. The CLV should not be confused with the "potential customer value", which is calculated from the total expenditure (including purchases from competitors) of the customer.

This can all be summarized under the term "Marketing Automation". It is a software-supported method for automating marketing processes. User profiles are enriched with information based on their user behavior in order to set up automated campaign processes for individual communication. Most of these software packages follow the "predictive lead scoring"[12] or so-called "lead nurturing." The lead-nurturing process begins with a search contact (inquiry). In the second step, the provider "nurtures" the contact by having the software establish a personal contact (Sales Accepted Lead/SAL). If the customer now indicates a willingness to buy, the company shows the prospective customer in detail what added value its products offer in particular (Sales Qualified Lead/SQL). In the fourth step, the purchase is concluded (Closed Won).[13]

---

[11] See Gernot Brauer, op. cit. p. 167.

[12] See Jennifer Weist, Predictive Lead Scoring: Looking into the Future is Present, in: OnlineMarketing.de from 29.07.2020.

[13] See Reinhard Janning, Lead Nurturing: A structured process for acquiring new customers, in: Online Marketing-Praxis.

Fig. 5.1 Nike's new machine-designed track shoe (Source: Nike Inc., Oregon)

But it is not only in connection with Big Data that AI has become indispensable for marketing. AI is also used for direct observation of customer behavior. Italian company A. Imax sells mannequins with computer vision and facial recognition software. Among other things, the Eysee mannequins observed that a particular group of customers preferred a particular entrance. The retail company responded by scheduling merchandise accordingly.[14] Since 2014, London-based technology company Iconeme has offered mannequins that communicate with customers via smartphone and provide customers with product information about the clothes they are trying on. In doing so, they also record information on age, gender and location, which outfit was looked at and whether a purchase was made or not.

The classic marketing functions also include the compilation of the product range. Here, AI opens up completely new possibilities in terms of product innovations. For example, with the help of algorithmic design software and a development time of four years, Nike has developed a running shoe for top athletes made of one piece, in which even the spikes are not screwed in, but integrated into the shoe shell using a 3D printing process (see Fig. 5.1). For a top athlete, according to the manufacturer, this shoe can achieve an improvement of one tenth of a second on the 100-m course, thus currently moving him forward from possibly fourth place to the gold medal.

Less AI-heavy are the personalized sneakers from Adidas, which are manufactured with batch size 1, so to speak, where a customer can select individual elements such as the shoe tongue, the logo, the stripes, the lining or the cap over the toes according to personal taste. In addition, Adidas and Nike are offering "do-it-yourself shoes" in line with the

---

[14] See Paul R. Daugherty/James Wilson, op. cit. p. 99.

increasingly demanding prosumers. Such individualized products follow the trend towards customization, i.e. the adaptation of series products to specific customer needs. The organic muesli from Mymuesli GmbH, where the customer can mix 566 quadrillion (!) variations according to the company, probably also falls into this category. McDonald's dynamic menu can also be subsumed under this category.

But AI not only enables customized product variants, but also entirely new products. The Carlsberg Group, for example, is brewing an "intelligent beer" with AI. High-tech sensors record the subtle nuances and aromas in the beer and create a "beer fingerprint" for each individual sample. This database is used to research novel beer yeasts to create new types of beer. The development of methods for the fast and reliable evaluation of flavours in complex mixtures such as in beer or other alcoholic and non-alcoholic beverages is of course of great interest for product development, quality control and safety. The English company IntelligentX makes use of this technology by evaluating customer feedback with an algorithm via a Facebook Messenger and adapting its four beer varieties accordingly on this basis. The customer thus becomes the "brewmaster".

It's only logical that other industries are using AI in similar ways. Philyra, for example, is an AI software including a huge database of 3000 raw materials that it uses to help perfumers create new fragrances. With this software, IBM and Symrise launched the first "computer perfumes" in 2019, evaluating 1.7 million chemical formulas.

The application of such technology can of course also be expected for the pharmaceutical and food industry. After all, the Vietnamese apple kebab does not fall from the tree, but was generated with Cognitive Cooking by "Chef" Watson. According to Mahmoud Naghshineh of IBM Research, "The idea of cognitive cooking is that machines and humans work together—in this case, a very complex analytical system that draws from extensive accumulated knowledge about chemistry, food culture, and taste preferences to help chefs break new ground."[15]

These examples show successful mass customization and prosumerism as two social trends that are supported by AI. The prosumer or prosumer—who is both consumer and producer—configures "customized innovations" according to his personal taste in an interactive co-creation with the "original manufacturer", whereby the latter thus engages in mimetic marketing by complying with social demands.

5.2 Touch Points Are Good, Conversions Are Better: AI in Sales and Service

Since sales and after sales management or service are strategically intertwined, both trade functions are treated together in this section.

---

[15] See https://www.ice.edu/partner-with-ice/IBM

A decisive sales criterion is without doubt the price. Online retailing has given rise to new forms of pricing.

One example is what is known as freemium, "a business model in which the basic product is offered for free, while the full product and add-ons are paid for. In the case of computer games, it is better known as free-to-play."[16] Another form of AI-based pricing design is "HiddenRevenue." This business model separates revenue and customers. By selling advertising space on the product, the product itself can often be given away to customers for free. A well-known example of this is Facebook, which is financed by ads rather than membership fees. For the company, this sales construct has the advantage of being able to tap into additional customers or sources of income by attracting customers who would not pay the real price.

At farmer's markets in developing countries, the author has often experienced touching "social pricing", in which the vegetable woman demanded a higher price from a recognisably wealthy person, than from the domestic servant standing next to him, who was thus able to get a few "pennies" on the side when settling accounts with the landlady. The flex price on the Internet has nothing to do with this social aspect; instead, the interdependence between supply and demand regulates the price rationally and objectively. Uber transport, for example, costs more at peak times, and the principle of maximising revenue by making prices more flexible applies to virtual airline ticket exchanges. This is dynamic pricing or surge pricing or dynamic price management, a pricing strategy in which companies adjust prices for products or services based on current market demand. Prices are calculated using automated algorithms, taking into account factors such as competitors' pricing, supply and demand, and other external factors.[17]

The author's kids common advice: "Don't buy on your first search. Wait first to see if you get a better offer without being asked." They are indirectly describing the "next best offer" principle—a type of personalized pricing that is automated by AI pricing software or algorithms. Up-selling " also involves an individualized offer, but in this case the customer is offered a higher-value product or service in the next step instead of a lower-priced variant, with reference to the advantages of the "uplift model". However, with this approach, there is a risk that the prospective buyer will not buy anything in the end because the intrusive up-selling is annoying.

This risk also exists in cross-selling, where the customer is encouraged to make additional purchases. This phenomenon is called "overkill targeting".[18]

Gamification "is also used to increase the propensity to convert. With playful elements such as high scores, progress bars, rankings, virtual goods or pseudo awards, purchase motivation and/or customer loyalty are to be increased.

---

[16] https://de.wikipedia.org/wiki/Freemium
[17] See Peter Gentsch, op. cit. p. 66.
[18] See Peter Gentsch, op. cit. p. 70.

Before we come to the new services in sales, the phenomenon of the "long tail" should be described here. While in the analogue economy the low-turnover C-products are sorted out with the ABC analysis, the virtual products in the online trade get their chance in the "long tail". Virtual goods have only marginal capital commitment costs and can thus remain in the assortment. Thus, specific demand groups that know about the versatile assortment can increasingly demand these niche products, which "thickens the tail" and thus makes them relevant for sales.

With AI, a number of new forms of sales support have emerged for trade. For example, trading with "smart contracts" can achieve high contract security, low transaction costs and process acceleration. "Curating shopping" is another AI-driven sales method. If the customer is willing to reveal their taste preferences, the "algorithmic style advisor" will send them garments to choose from. What the "responsible" (?) consumer doesn't like, he simply sends back.[19]

Chat bots have already been mentioned several times, but especially in retail we have to come back to them. Because here they play an increasingly claimed role as patient and ever-present sales consultants. For example, the bot from KIK in collaboration with H&M makes suggestions for clothing when the customer fills out a corresponding question-naire.[20] And such recommendation bots can also be found at Burberry, Hilfiger and other fashion companies. The "LoweBot" of the DIY chain Lowe drives around in DIY stores to answer customer questions or to "intelligently" check stock levels.

At Lidl, a chatbot advises customers on wine purchases. And that brings us to AI in offline retail. In the networked fitting room, for example, you can generate styling suggestions by entering the barcode of items of clothing on a touchscreen or ask the sales assistant to bring the item in a different size or colour. If the booth also has a "smart mirror", it can pass on details about the products, simulate different lighting situations such as daylight or sunset, and make customer-specific dressing suggestions.[21]

But AI has help available not only for bots, but also for "real" salespeople. The company Cogito, for example, gives call center employees recommendations on how to conduct conversations by comparing and analyzing factors such as volume, pauses in conversation, voice pitch, etc. with successful calls (look-and-feel).[22] For chatbots, this is offered by the Chinese company "emotibot", which promises to improve the efficiency of service robots in the call center with "emotion recognition".

Predictive analysis "by software specialists such as Blue Yonder or Tableau, which take weather conditions, holidays and many other criteria into account in their sales forecasts,

---

[19] See Thomas Ramge, op. cit. p. 58.
[20] See Paul R. Daugtherty/H. James Wilson, op. cit., p. 101.
[21] See Christoph Keese, op. cit. p. 98.
[22] See Andreas Wagener, op. cit. p. 144.

guarantees the freshness of products in offline retailing because the range of products is precisely matched to changing demand.[23]

It is remarkable that the large online retailer Amazon is now also successful in offline retail with AmazonGo. The company is trying to create a new shopping experience. The extreme freshness of the food is permanently controlled by means of special cameras and there is no waiting at the checkout because sensors and cameras have previously recorded the purchased goods so that they are automatically calculated when leaving the store. However, this requires the customer to have an Amazon profile and download the Amazon Go app, which is certainly not detrimental to customer loyalty. Similarly, at Dutch discounter HEMA, customers get the sensory experience of offline retail with the freshest merchandise while also enjoying the convenience of online sales.

Convenient mobile payment methods are offered by Apple Pay, Samsung Pay, WeChat, Microsoft Wallet and Apple Wallet, which can be used for online purchases as well as for "real-world" shopping.

Big Data provides offline retail with suggestions for "nudging", i.e. giving customers the impetus to make "good" purchases. It has been proven, for example, that fruit is more often preferred to pastries at canteen buffets if it is presented within easy reach. In this context, one also speaks somewhat jokingly of "libertarian paternalism" when, for example, a "veggie day" is proclaimed.

Once the online purchase has been virtually completed after all the seduction components, the goods still have to reach the customer in the same way. And with today's demand for "immediacy", the delivery time can become a not insignificant competitive advantage. This is where predictive logistics comes into play. Amazon is already experimenting with "anticipatory logistics" by distributing goods to decentralized warehouses on the basis of sales forecasts even before the actual sale of goods.

Together with IBM, logistics company Maersk launched TradeLens in 2018. TradeLens is a networked blockchain system of cargo owners, maritime and inland shipping companies, freight forwarders and logistics providers, ports and terminals, customs authorities and more to make international freight transport more efficient. For the fleet association of a logistics company, the in-house use of a floating car data system (FCD), which informs about the location and condition of vehicles in use, but also about congestion, availability of waiting spaces and other traffic events, is also very helpful.

For the last step in the supply chain, there are also already attempts to improve this shipping phase with AI. Amazon, for example, wants to achieve "instantness" with drones. The fully automated "Prime Air" aircraft promises a delivery time of no more than 30 min. With the robots "Baxter" and "Sawyer" from Rethink Robotics, DHL not only optimizes the processes in their warehouses, but also improves the delivery to the customer with "Smart Trucking". And the delivery service Hermes is attempting human-free delivery

---

[23] See Genor Brauer, op. cit. p. 27.

from the parcel shop to the end customer with small Starship delivery robots in a 15-min time window freely selectable by the recipient.

Keeping in mind the already rapidly increasing innovations in retail, one will agree with Gläß, the founder of GK Software, that "the development of a special AI, namely an "Artificial Retail Intelligence", is necessary for retail."[24]

One area of trade that is essential for the economy as a whole, namely the financial sector, under which we also subsume the insurance industry here, has been left out so far in order to consider it separately from an AI perspective in the next section.

5.3 Econometrics or Wheel of Fortune: AI in the Financial Sector

The author has been advising banks on their human resources issues for decades. During this time, he was repeatedly approached about the search for investment bankers. There was obviously a supply deficit for this job profile, which led to astonishing income opportunities, especially at the turn of the millennium. To this day, the author has not understood why, despite the pecuniary pull factor, there has not been a balance between supply and demand over these many years. All the more so as he was familiar with the following anecdote: the PR manager of an investment house threw plenty of pieces of bread to the camels in Frankfurt Zoo, which were labelled with the names of shares. He put together a virtual fund of the shares eaten by the animals and followed their price development over a considerable period of time, during which he was able to prove that the fund managers of his prestigious house did not achieve better results. Wisely, he didn't exploit this finding in PR terms, but at least there was a timely swelling of "unmanaged" index funds. And the call for investment bankers has since faded as well.

This is also not surprising, because Goldman Sachs, for example, once had about 600 stock traders in securities trading and asset management, and today allegedly only two.[25] It wouldn't be surprising, since much of the stock market trading is now done through "algotrade," or automated trading with computer programs. In "high frequency trading", which is of course automated in order to achieve high stock exchange turnover with short holding times, it is now not only the quality of the algorithms that is crucial to success, but also—at least for trading in the microsecond range—the length and strength of the line to the stock exchange has become an essential competitive factor. The extent to which the algorithms of the trading institutions are similar in their conception and simplicity in reacting to exceptional situations can be seen in the flash crashes that occur from time to time, in which the price crash can often only be slowed down by suspending trading.

---

[24] Rainer Gläß, Artificial Intelligence in Retailing, Wiesbaden, 2018, p. 27.
[25] Gernot Brauer, op. cit. p. 143.

What used to be arbitrage by carrier pigeons is now AI, with which industrial developments of individual regions are picked up via satellite images in order to invest in so-called "quantamentel funds".[26]

When the smart Bill Gates said back in 1994: "Banking is necessary, banks are not", the experts were still amused. Today, the bank-specific robo-advisors such as SEB's "Amelia", Bank of America's "Erica" or the savings banks' "Linda" are still advising customers, but the major internet platforms have already taken over a significant proportion of payment transactions. And Bitcom will not have a monopoly position as a cryptocurrency for much longer; it is to be expected that GAFA will also soon make use of the secure blockchain technology for its own currency systems.

It is true that the banks have already largely automated loan approval and processing and thus, among other things, noticeably reduced the credit risk. But private "crowd funding"is already looming, which doesn't have to worry about such cumbersome regulations as Basel I through V. Alibaba does not have to observe these either when it grants its microloans of up to 150,000 € without human intervention.[27]

For banks and insurance companies, IBM offers the "Security Trusteer" program, a software that uses cloud-based AI to automatically detect fraud and verify new customers (fraud prevention and authentication).

AI offers further outstanding potential for the insurance industry. While a life insurance policy can take a long time to be concluded in the traditional way, the US company Lapetus makes it possible with its "Chronos" software to calculate the life expectancy of the potential policyholder by taking a selfie and answering nine questions, in order to formulate an insurance offer in a matter of seconds.

In claims settlement, AI not only leads to a significant reduction in staff and costs, but also to an increased detection of insurance fraud cases by way of pattern recognition with Big Data. Algorithms also handle the assessment of claims faster and more accurately than claims handlers, which is a noticeable advantage for liquidity planning. In the medium term, systems such as Munich Re's Early Loss Detection (ELD) programme, which draws geocoded risk and loss information from more than 16,000 news sources, will be even more important in order to be able to initiate appropriate measures in claims management at an early stage.

IBM's Watson Complaint Analysis system handles much of the correspondence with insurance customers and is now even able to recognize irony in customer letters and respond accordingly.[28]

The extent to which AI will continue to drive "dehumanisation" in the financial sector will be considered in more detail in Chap. 8.

---

[26] See Martin Ford, op. cit. p. 133.

[27] See Andrea Cornelius, op. cit., p. 45 ff.

[28] See Gernot Brauer, op. cit. p. 148 f.

Where to Go with the "Social Fallow"?: Industry 4.0

6

> *One machine can do the work of fifty ordinary men, but it cannot replace one extraordinary one.*
> *Elbert Hubbard.*

In former times, there were enough village idiots—they had to herd geese or do other intellectually undemanding work. It is not known that there are less stupid people nowadays (even if the helicopter parents perceive their brats as highly gifted, whose genius is only not recognized by demotivated teachers), but industry 4.0 offers no more stupid jobs. What to do with the "social fallow"?—It is no coincidence that the call for an unconditional basic income (precaution 4.0) is becoming more and more audible.

6.1 "One Two Three" and 4.0?: Ontology of Industry 4.0

"Industry 4.0"—of course the educated engineer knows immediately that this is the new industrial era after 3.x.x, because this is how software developments are coded with the usual version numbering. In the case of decisive changes, one speaks of a new version, whereby the first digit of the version number (= major version number) is increased by one and at the same time the second digit (= minor version number) is reset to zero. With the 0 (after the 4), Hennig Kagermann, Wolf-Dieter Lukas and Wolfgang Wahlster, the "fathers of Industry 4.0", wanted to express in 2011 at the Hannover Messe that the fourth "industrial revolution" is still in its early stages. Even if this cryptic meaning is likely to remain inaccessible to the uninitiated layman, he will nevertheless be able to conclude: Where there is a 4.0, there must have been a 3.0, and indeed a 2.0 and 1.0,

© Springer Fachmedien Wiesbaden GmbH, part of Springer Nature 2021
G. Cisek, *The Triumph of Artificial Intelligence*,
https://doi.org/10.1007/978-3-658-34896-0_6

before that.—Wrong! It must be confessed that industry 1.0 to 3.0 were at least conceptually "calved" only after 4.0 and are defined as follows:

- "The **first industrial revolution** consisted in **mechanization** by means of water and steam power; it was followed by
- the **second industrial revolution**, characterized by **mass production** with the help of assembly lines and electrical energy, and subsequently
- the **third industrial revolution** or digital revolution with the use of electronics and IT (especially programmable logic control) to **automate** production."[1]

Certainly, the alternative term "intelligent factory"[2] or the Anglo-Saxon version "smart factory"is more meaningful to the layperson than the abstract term "Industry 4.0", but neither are these versions more accurate. "Smart" is too anthropomorphic for a factory, and "intelligent" in the factory so far are at best the people who intelligently design the algorithms that make the industrial process "smart". Probably the term "**digital networked economy**" would be most appropriate for what is really shaping the essential transformation of industry. After all, if the essential features of Industry 4.0 are presented below, it will become clear that this is accompanied by a massive transformation of the entire economic life and thus the term actually falls short. But let's stick with "Industry 4.0", especially since this term has obviously become established with "Retail 4.0", "Medicine 4.0", "Learning 4.0" or "Office 4.0". The question is whether one should lament that with all the 4 Zeros for human existence, it has so far only been enough for "Life 3.0".[3]

Let us now turn to the substantive definition of "Industrie 4.0" or the "*Industrie du futur*", as it is called in France. According to the Frauenhofer Institute, Industry 4.0 "stands for the intelligent networking of product development, production, logistics and customers."[4] The Industrie 4.0 working group understands this to mean "a networking of autonomous, situationally self-controlling, self-configuring, knowledge-based, sensor-supported and spatially distributed production resources (production machines, robots, conveyor and storage systems, operating resources), including their planning and control systems."[5] Or, as Andreas Syska and Philippe Lievre put it quite comprehensibly: "In highly simplified terms, Industry 4.0 is the web-based networking of technical objects in the factory and across its product life cycle."[6]

---

[1] https://de.wikipedia.org/wiki/Industrie_4.0

[2] Christian Manzei/Linus Schleupner/Ronald Heinze (eds.), Industrie 4.0 im internationalen Kontext, Berlin, 2016, p. 11.

[3] Tegmark, Max, Leben 3.0, Mensch sein im Zeitalter Künstlicher Intelligenz, Berlin, 2017.

[4] https://www.fraunhofer.de/de/forschung/forschungsfelder/produktion-dienstleistung/industrie-4-0.html

[5] Günther Reinhart, Handbuch Industrie 4.0, Munich, 2017, p. 18.

[6] Andreas Syska/Philippe Lievre, Illusion 4.0, Germany's naive dream of the smart factory, Herrieden, 2016, p. 61.

Essential in Industry 4.0 is therefore the digital networking of the entire value chain from product development to customer service. Henry Ford could still sneer: "Any customer can get his car painted any color he wants, as long as the color is black." By the early 1960s, that was already over, and marketing moved to a market-oriented corporate strategy. But the market then was still an amorphous crowd of customers who were fobbed off with mass-produced goods. With Industry 4.0, on the other hand, we have the "personalized" customer who is served with batch size 1 or is even involved as a "prosumer" in the sense of mimetic marketing in product development and manufacturing.[7]

If you want to get an idea of what is changing with this fourth industrial revolution, you have to take a closer look at the four defining characteristics of the innovation process: Cyper-physical systems (CPS), the "smart workpiece", hybrid teams and the entrepreneurial accompaniment of the "product life circle" or the digitally networked value creation process.

A cyber-physical system is a network of IT and software components with mechanical and electronic parts that communicate via a data infrastructure such as the Internet.[8] The name already indicates the two-dimensionality of the system. Parallel to the physical-real components, there is also a completely identical virtual image. One of the basic technologies that make such a data-rich link between real and virtual existence possible is technical sensor technology for measuring and controlling processes and workpieces. Sensors convert non-electrical measured variables into electrical signals, while as counterparts actuators are used as moving parts of robots, which after all play a crucial role in Industry 4.0, for sensor positioning and orientation.[9] A technical innovation for this is the transmitter-receiver system "radio-frequency identification" (RFID), the "identification with the help of electromagnetic waves". With this technology, living beings and objects can be automatically and contactlessly identified and located via a reader, provided they carry a coded transponder or radio label. In 2006, researchers at the Fraunhofer Institute for Manufacturing Technology and Advanced Materials (IFAM) in Bremen succeeded for the first time in casting temperature-insensitive RFID transponders into metallic components made of light metal. This process development makes it possible to integrate the RFID transponders directly into the component during component manufacture using a die-casting process. (The "digital twin" or the "intelligent workpiece" is actually a subset of this CPS, but will be described later as a second independent characteristic due to its novelty and central systemic significance).

In order to be able to actually use this process in practice, one needs the "Internet der Dinge" (IdD), whereby the English term "Internet of Things" (IoT) is also more common in Germany. This "all-network" stands for technologies of a global infrastructure of the information society, which makes it possible to network physical and virtual objects with each other and to let people cooperate with each other by networked electronic systems as

---

[7] See Günther Reinhart, op. cit.

[8] See Ralf Otte, op. cit. p. 309; Walter Simon, op. cit. p. 92.

[9] See Günther Reinhart, op. cit., p. 323 f.

Fig. 6.1 Digital twin from Siemens for pump operation (Photo: Siemens AG)

well as systems through information and communication technologies.[10] It remains to be seen when the 5G rollout will enable us to fully embrace the IoT.

Regardless of the resilience of our Internet, however, one innovation of Industry 4.0 is already real as a special feature: the "Digital Twin". The "digital twin" is the "digital representation" of a material object. It may well be that this object does not yet exist in real terms, but is still in product development as a virtual model. This results in a considerable advantage, because it makes physical prototypes unnecessary. In this context, one also speaks of "Digital Mock Up" (DMU). This is a computer-generated test model that is as realistic as possible and is used primarily to replace cost-intensive product testing with computer simulations.

Digital twins enable an overarching exchange of data that also allows the virtual simulation of the object's functionality and its progression through the production process (see Fig. 6.1). For production companies, the digital twin with its integrated services can be a decisive competitive advantage, as the new business models will show in the next section.

In addition to these "object twins", there are also twins for entire production facilities, processes and services. The different digital twins can be linked to each other and also allow extensive communication and interaction with the real twins. This is then referred to

---

[10] See Luis de Miranda (ed.), Artificial Intelligence & Robotics in 30 Seconds, Visions, Challenges & Risks, Vilnius, 2019, p. 132; Christiana Köhler-Schute, Industrie 4.0: Ein praxisorientierter Ansatz, Berlin, 2015, p. 21 ff; Holger Kern, Architekturen für das "Internet der Dinge", in: Christian Manzei/ Linus Schleupner/Ronald Heinze (eds.), op. cit, p. 30; Thomas Schulz (ed.), Industrie 4.0, Potenziale erkennen und umsetzen, 1st ed., Würzburg, 2017, p. 7.

Fig. 6.2 Human-robot collaboration (HRC) (Source: KUKA "Human-Robot Collaboration (MRC)")

as a "digital thread",[11] which possibly runs through the entire product life cycle like a "digital shadow".[12]

The number of IoT endpoints will increase by billions worldwide. Digital twins will become an essential component of intelligent digitalization and significantly advance numerous cross-industry megatrends such as the "Internet of Things", "Industry 4.0", "Connected Home" or "Smart City". Their potential use goes far beyond current production and logistics applications. In the USA, this is also referred to as "ambient intelligence". Digital twins could decisively drive the digital transformation of society if the corresponding network capacities and the necessary amount of energy were available.

The third characteristic of Industrie 4.0 is "hybrid teams", which will be discussed again in the next section on the production process. They are composed of humans, robots, software-based assistance systems and intelligent virtual environments (see Fig. 6.2). The collaborative use between humans and robots without separating protective devices has become possible since the safety sensor technology of the "digital servants" with position, speed, force and moment monitoring, collision detection and orientation monitoring guarantees collision avoidance. Kuka explains: "The human controls and monitors the

---

[11] See Günther Reinhart, op. cit. p. 9.

[12] See Günther Reinhart, op. cit. p. 113.

production, the robot takes over the physically demanding work. Both contribute their specific skills: a crucial principle of Industry 4.0."[13]

In this way, the strengths of humans and robots are synergistically combined. The concept also goes by the abbreviation MTO (Man-Technology-Organization), but in the author's opinion it is rather a very general dimensioning of operational systems.[14]

As the fourth substantial element of Industrie 4.0, we have listed above the entrepreneurial accompaniment of the entire product cycle. The Industrie 4.0 working group recommends "digital engineering throughout the entire product lifecycle" as the key to the successful implementation of an Industrie 4.0 strategy. This is also referred to as "Product Lifecycle Management" (PLM).[15] We will discuss this in more detail in the next section.

6.2   "Panta rei": The Value Creation Process in Industry 4.0

The PLM concept of Industrie 4.0 roughly structures the value chain into vertical and horizontal integration. The product life phases include:

- Idea-to-Offer: Product creation
- Offer-to-order: product distribution
- Order-to-Delivery: Product manufacturing (the actual value creation)
- Delivery-to-Customer Care: product delivery and service.

Vertical integration here means that not only does the entire production process take place within the company, but that it also continues after delivery of the product through services via new business models.

In Industrie 4.0, horizontal integration is understood to mean both cross-manufacturer development work, such as joint research by different car manufacturers on fuel cells in the sense of "coopetition" (duality of competition and cooperation), as well as internal company integration with AI-optimized material and information flows of different organizational units at the same level.[16]

For better clarity, the value creation process is now presented according to the levels of the "automation pyramid", as it has been structured since the 1990s based on the OSI model (Open Systems Interconnection Model)—a reference model for network protocols as layered architecture (see Fig. 6.3).

So let's start at the field level, which is also referred to as the sensor and actuator level. At the "real-physical" level, sensors, probes, photoelectric sensors and switches are used to

---

[13] https://www.kuka.com/de-de/future-production/mensch-roboter-kollaboration
[14] See Günther Reinhart, op. cit. p. 54.
[15] See Ulrich Eberl, op. cit. p 213.
[16] See Christiana Köhler-Schute, op. cit. p. 19.

Fig. 6.3 Automation pyramid

collect data such as the fill level, temperature, speeds and pressure, as well as safety and quality-relevant process data. A frequently used bus is the Profibus—a standardized, manufacturer-independent fieldbus for industrial automation and manufacturing technology—which is used to feed peripheral units such as I/O modules (input/output actuators), measuring transducers, the control units for valves and motors, and the operator consoles of the administrators. The data is usually acquired using the concept of Supervisory Control and Data Acquisition (SCADA), which is used to control and monitor the technical processes. Here, the fuzzy logic described in Chap. 3 is often used for the measurement methods.

These components described above, which are provided with "embedded intelligence" or function as molded interconnect devices (3D-MID = injection-molded circuit carriers with applied metallic conductor paths),[17] must process small amounts of data at high speed, so that the real-time problem must already be taken into account here at this level. The TSN method is used for this purpose, whereby the sensor-actuator network is divided into "traffic classes" with different time windows with "hard" and "soft" real-time conditions for the communication speed. At the field level, decentralized "edge computing"[18] is largely used to process the data directly at the end devices, the Micro-Electro-Mechanical Systems (MEMS), in a memory-saving manner. Edge computing is often mistakenly equated with "fog computing". Fog computing does indeed also take place decentrally at the "edge", i.e. at the end devices, but not in order to communicate the data internally to the next level, but rather to communicate it to the "cloud" for the users.

---

[17] See Günther Reinhart, op. cit. p. 654.

[18] See Thomas Schulz, op. cit. p. 72, p. 208 ff.

The fieldbus transports the data from the field level to the control and monitoring level. At this level, the processes of production or manufacturing/assembly are digitally recorded and monitored in near real time. Complex Event Processing (CEP) is used for the data that must be delivered in real time. At the control level, the production machines/plants are controlled via the programmable logic controller (PLC). The production process is controlled and regulated by analyzing and evaluating sensor data from the field level, the results of which are fed back with actuator control.[19] In addition to PLCs, IC controls (integrated circuits, i.e. microcontrollers) and PC controls (control by the microprocessor) are also widespread.

This is not a gradual but an essential change in the production process. In classic production, the workpiece was only subjected to quality control - if at all - after the completion of a production phase and was often only identified as a reject in the final inspection. In Industry 4.0, the production control system "supervises" the workpiece continuously in "real time" and automatically regulates almost every deviation from the standard channel, so that a final inspection is actually unnecessary. Given the large number of variables (e.g. when pressing a car roof, the sensor system works with over 30 predictors such as sheet thickness, degree of oiling, roughness, stability,

lifting speed, various press pressures, etc.), this production process was only made possible by Moore's Law, which is still valid, and which made the huge storage capacity required for this technically possible and affordable.

Not only are "intelligent", i.e. AI-supported processes, systems and tools increasingly found at the field and control level, but the "intelligent workpieces" are also implemented here as a result. In the concept of Industry 4.0, products or workpieces undergo a paradigm shift that includes not only the manufacturing process but also the later use phase, in which the workpiece can continue to actively communicate with the user and manufacturer.[20] This will be explained in more detail below in the presentation of new business models. But it should already be pointed out here that this "intelligent" property is a compelling basis for "predictive maitenance".

The management and control level also bears the designation "motion level". It is often also referred to as the "process management level" above the control and monitoring level. Here we find the already mentioned hybrid teams or HRK (human-robot collaboration) workplaces. With the latest technology, employees now control the "collaborative" robots "by voice" and soon also "by mind", because the robot will be able to read the thoughts of the employees.[21] Today, at least, it can learn its task not by programming, but by imitating the gestures of its team "colleagues". One of the best-known of these HRC teams is ABB's YuMi ("you and me—we work together"). The use of such hybrid teams requires a

---

[19] See Günther Reinhart, op. cit. p. 555 ff.

[20] See Günther Reinhart, op. cit. p. 255.

[21] See Michio Kaku, Physics of the future, The Inventions that will transform our lives, London, 2012, p. 112.

resource-oriented architecture (ROA) for the process-related connection of heterogeneous cyber-physical systems and IT environments.

However, the human teams in production are not only supported by robots. Anyone who has to lift heavy things is certainly grateful for robotic prostheses. "Smart glasses" (data glasses) with "augmented reality" show the assembler three-dimensionally how to assemble the workpiece and tell the mechatronics engineer which inputs to type into the CNC machine. With a "remote eye tracker", the production engineer can take non-contact measurements on the screen. And SafetyEye safeguards danger points with its 3D camera system.

Let's now move on to the plant management level, where detailed production planning, production data acquisition, KPI determination, material management and quality management take place, i.e. the value creation process and the necessary resources are planned and its actual execution is controlled and monitored. For this purpose, instead of the traditional Manufacturing Execution System (MES), the AI-founded MES and Management Information Systems (MIT) are now available. More appropriate and comprehensive is the system "Collaborative Production Management" (CPM), because it includes a "collaborative" cooperation of production with the production peripheral areas such as purchasing, procurement, controlling and logistics. It seems important to the author to highlight this AI-backed process, integrated across all stages of value creation, as typical of Industrie 4.0. It also makes a lot of sense to closely link the material flow with the production process in terms of supply chain management (SCM). It goes without saying that "intelligent" floor driving technology, i.e. automated guided vehicles (AGVs), are used nowadays and that the transported goods are stored under AI control in "chaotic warehousing" and the stored goods are moved with Pick2Voice or Move-by-voice (= voice picking as a "paperless" picking process).[22] When Precht laments: "The storage of goods at Amazon has an arrangement logic that is hardly comprehensible to humans and can only be mastered with the help of a pocket computer[23]"he only shows that he has not yet heard of this storage principle, which has been practiced everywhere for decades even without AI.

At the top level of the automation pyramid, top management makes corporate strategy decisions that, while AI-assisted by MIS cockpits and "enterprise resource planning" (ERP) systems, are hopefully made primarily with "natural intelligence." AI remains relevant here, especially in new business models, which will be explained in a moment.

First of all, however, it must be asked how Industry 4.0 is to be established in the company in the first place. There are usually two approaches to this in the literature, namely the:

1. Greenfield approach, in which the Industrie 4.0 facility is newly created on a "greenfield" site, such as the BMW logistics center currently planned in Dingolfing

---

[22] This has nothing to do with "pig economy", but it means that the stored goods do not have a fixed storage location, but are stored in a coded manner where there is space. This reduces the required storage space considerably.

[23] Richard David Precht, op. cit. p. 219.

2. Brownfield approach, in which existing plants are converted to Industry 4.0 step by step ("retrofitting") - apparently the most chosen path at present.[24]

Reinhart describes yet a third, but inconsistent and apparently unusual way with the Grass Blade approach: "In the Grass Blade approach, the existing technical-organizational environment of the old generation is largely retained and merely supplemented or replaced by selected elements of the new generation."[25] The term seems a bit unfortunate. The industrially uninformed layman like the author would rather assume: "The excavator is coming!" and "mows away" the oldjunk.

But now finally to the new business models that were only made possible by AI. Perhaps the Business Model Canvas is a helpful "creative tableau" for developing new business ideas, but since it has nothing to do with AI, it is left out here. In contrast, the models of cloud computing are presented below.

For a better understanding, cloud computing and the different cloud variants must first be introduced. Cloud computing is an IT infrastructure that makes storage space, computing power or application software available as a service via the Internet without having to be installed on the service customer's local computer. These services are offered and used exclusively via technical interfaces and protocols, for example by means of a web browser.

The service user can choose from the following cloud variants:

Public cloud—the public computer cloud.

It offers the general public access to IT infrastructures via the Internet. Payment is made according to actual use (pay-as-you-go). The advantage for (mostly private) users is that they do not have to invest in computer and data centre infrastructure.

Private cloud—the private computer cloud.

The private cloud is operated exclusively for an organization. Hosting and management of the cloud platform can be done internally (for example, by the company's own data centers), but also by third parties. As already mentioned, mainly large companies and companies with large IT requirements use this service. Arguably the most successful cloud in this regard is Microsoft Azure. The installation of a 'private cloud' is also carried out under data protection and security aspects, especially for high-tech companies.

Hybrid cloud—the hybrid computing cloud.

This is a combination of public and private cloud where the service user differentiates the usage according to their different needs.

Community cloud—the collaborative computing cloud.

This is a quasi-public cloud with a limited user community of mostly local or regional user communities such as government agencies, universities or research teams, or business associations.

Furthermore, there are hybrid forms of the above cloud types:

---

[24] See Günther Reinhart, op. cit., p. 214 ff; Thomas Schulz, op. cit., p. 113; Christiana Köhler-Schute, op. cit., p. 37.

[25] Günther Reinhart, op. cit. p. 214.

The **virtual private cloud** is a private computer cloud on IT infrastructures of the public cloud that are in principle publicly accessible. The "privatization" takes place through special compartmentalization mechanisms.

The **multi-cloud** is a bundling of different cloud computing services. The Multi Cloud enables the parallel use of cloud services and platforms from several providers. The user uses it like a single large cloud. Basically, it is a further development of the **hybrid cloud**, where several cloud computing services can be used simultaneously in a heterogeneous system architecture.

Cloud computing gives rise to business models of varying intensity. A first, innovative business model is called "Software as a Service" (**SaaS**), which deposits a completely new relationship between customer and manufacturer. Just as Airbnb does not own airplanes or Uber does not own cars, but acts as a quasi-holo organization with only its software, in the SaaS model the customer only becomes the possesor, but not the owner of what he has "purchased". The service recipient also no longer pays for the object, but only for its use (pay per use). There are different forms of usage measurement. With "pay per GB", only the gigabytes used for cloud usage, for example, are charged, and with "pay per event", only the "event" that is accessed is charged.

In this context, it is worth mentioning the operator models, which are characterized by the fact that they no longer sell their hardware, but a service package around their product. For example, with Rolls-Royce, the airlines no longer buy the turbines, but their use as well as their "predictive" and "prescriptive maintenance"[26] and periodic software updates. Similarly, elevator manufacturers are now supplying a cloud-based online service with the turbines, enabling "tele-repairs" in "real time". Even Käser no longer sells its compressors, but only compressed air as a service.[27] And we have already heard from the agricultural industry that it not only provides machines, but also cloud-based service platforms that largely control the sowing, fertilizing and harvesting process.

Another business variant is "Platform as a Service" (**PaaS**). Here, the provider makes available a platform (including micro services such as authentication, IT security, etc.), with whose cloud infrastructure the programs and applications can then be used in the sense of a SaaS. The service user has the advantage that he not only outsources huge storage capacity, but also "does not have to develop and stock commodity development and operating software and the communication technology between applications/users himself". Not only is this offering very attractive to the mid-market, as you can imagine, but large global enterprises are slowly catching on and are now happy to take advantage of this service. Thus, PaaS is the middle layer in the "cloud stack".

---

[26] While "predictive maintenance" uses stream-based control to predict events, "prescriptive maintenance" uses predefined solution patterns proactively as soon as significant deviations from the norm occur.

[27] See Bettina Volkens, op. cit., p. 51; Andreas Syska/Philippe Lievre, op. cit., p. 141 ff.

With "Infrastructure as a Service" (**IaaS**), the company leases the required infrastructure such as storage space (i.e. hard disks) and network components—essentially the hardware. This is why this service offering is sometimes also referred to as "Hardware as a Service" (**HaaS**).

As a final step, a service user can also book "Everything as a Service" (**EaaS** or **XaaS**), where in addition to software, runtime environments and hardware, other desired services—in other words, "everything"—are also provided.

To ensure that the many clouds do not develop into dangerous thunderstorms, it is necessary to agree on overarching system and security standards, as illustrated in the next section.

6.3   YU-MI & Internet of Everything (IoET): Industry 4.0 Networked and Secure

In the Internet of Everything, not only are laptops, smartphones and other wearables connected to each other as in the classic Internet, but also intelligent machines and hybrid teams such as YuMi as well as all the networking services. If the digital transformation of industrial production in the sense of integral Industry 4.0 is to function within the framework of these unmanageable mountains of data, it is highly advisable to agree on a set of rules among themselves to ensure the global exchange of data in a compatible manner.

For the Federal Republic of Germany, the ZVEI, together with the VDI/VDE and partners from Bitkom and VDMA, has undertaken such a standardization and developed the reference architecture model RAMI 4.0. It serves companies as a three-dimensional basic structure for the development of products, processes and business models. The Rami cube has the process stages as one dimension, as we already know them from the automation pyramid. Parallel to this, the hierarchy levels are defined on the next dimension, as they are summarized in the automation pyramid with the process levels. The third dimension contains the product cycle and value creation process as a time vector (see Fig. 6.4).

A basic prerequisite for Industrie 4.0 participants to understand and communicate with each other is the unambiguous mirroring of the "gentelligent" systems and workpieces. This is done for the objects in accordance with the twin standard IEC 61360, which is used to fully describe the technical data element types. These items are referred to as "assets" to express that they are valuable to the enterprise.

However, it is not enough to "describe an asset only with characteristics". Each asset has certain technical functions and special properties that are described in the layers of RAMI 4.0 and characterize its actual purpose of use. For this purpose, this functionality must be formally described and available for machine processing. The formal description can be done with a suitable "language" or with executable code available in a library.

On the product lifecycle axis, the asset's lifecycle file is kept and its assignment to the corresponding instance on the hierarchy levels is continuously updated.

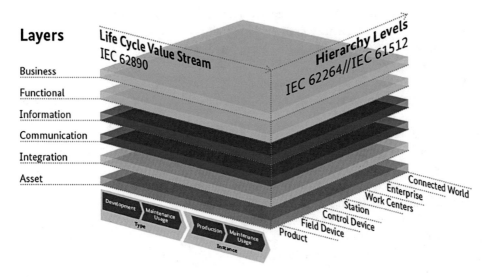

Fig. 6.4 Rami 4.0

The "management shell" is of central importance here. It is the digital implementation of the "digital twin" for Industry 4.0. On the one hand, it guarantees its "virtual representation" and describes its "technical functionality" on the other. With 4.0-compliant APIs (Application Programming Interface), it creates cross-manufacturer interoperability and maps the entire life cycle for products, devices and machinery.

In this context it should be added: What RAMI 4.0 is for Germany, OPC UA (Open Platform Communications United Architecture) is for the world, i.e. a global standard for data exchange with platform-independent, service-oriented architecture (SOA).

With cloud computing, there are of course legitimate concerns about data protection and security. IEC 62 44-3-3 plays a key role in this context. IEC 62443 is an international series of standards that tracks the cybersecurity of industrial automation and control systems (IACS) for operators, integrators and manufacturers. It provides them with standards, codes of practice and technical reports to help them design, control and implement processes securely. This is intended to reduce the risk of compromised information or production downtime.[28]

Despite various control mechanisms such as access, transfer, input or order control and the separation of data for different purposes, the security barriers are also successfully overcome time and again. These criminal attempts are supported by extortion software (ransomware) such as "Exploit as a Service" (**EaaS**). Some of these hackers must be credited with only wanting to expose security vulnerabilities with the exploit so that the software manufacturer will close the security hole. Microsoft is even said to be counting on such nerds to have their programs perfected by the "customer" at low cost.

---

[28] See Thomas Schulz, op. cit. p. 138.

But in addition to the "well-intentioned", there are above all many who want to maliciously exploit the data network.

Only some of the illegal attack methods are listed here:

- **Content spoofing**
  The end user is led to believe that he is on a reputable website with the intention of obtaining his information.
- **Cross-site scripting (XSS)**
  Malicious code is injected into a web application, which is then unknowingly executed by other users.
- **Denial of service**
  Malicious service blocking by a concentrated attack on the servers or other components of the data network in order to overload them
- **Tampering**
  Manipulation or editing of data through unauthorized channels
- **Phishing**
  Identity theft through fake websites, emails or text messages (it's like fishing: You don't know what's going to bite, but eventually you'll have something on the line).
- **Elevation of privilege**
  Procuring unauthorised access
- **Drive-by infection**
  with prepared websites on the Internet, the malware is automatically downloaded by calling up such a website.[29]

Unfortunately, according to the BKA (Federal Criminal Police Office), cybercrime is on the rise. According to a Bitkom study from 2017, every second Internet user was a victim of cybercrime. Although the rate will be significantly lower for industrial cloud computing, the damage to German industry still amounts to around 22.4 billion euros per year, according to Bitkom calculations.[30]

This chapter didn't really deserve this somewhat sinister ending, but it was unavoidable due to the thematic sequence.

Let us now turn to the social implications of AI.

---

[29] See Thomas Schulz, op. cit. p. 311 f.

[30] Tillmann Braun, Cybercrime costs German companies over 22 billion euros, in: ZDNet, 23.12.2016.

How Is Our Togetherness Changing?: Social Implications of AI

> *A prognosticator is a man who has gloomy forebodings in bright moments.*
> *Tennessee Williams*

Artificial Intelligence has, of course, already had a noticeable impact on social life. And Marr states categorically: "One thing is absolutely clear: Artificial Intelligence (AI) will change the world once and for all."[1]

One only has to think of the astounding successes in medicine, the dramatic increase in online commerce or the exuberant digital communication in social media. And yet we must assume that we are only at the beginning of these developments and that the AI-related essential changes to society speculated about in this chapter are yet to come.

7.1 Where Does the Sharpened Income Gap Lead?: The Modern Welfare State

Already since the end of the war the income gap in Germany has widened disproportionately, without the AI being to blame for this. The culprit so far has been the unfair collective bargaining policy, which always agrees the same percentage increase for all pay scale groups. This leads, of course, not to a linear but to a proportional spread, which, after more than 70 years on the time vector, is hardly mitigated even by base amounts for the lower pay scale groups. Three percent of e.g. 6043 € in wage group 17 of the metal and electrical

---

[1] Bernard Marr, Artificial Intelligence in Business, Innovative Applications in 50 Successful Companies, Weinheim 2020, p. 9.

© Springer Fachmedien Wiesbaden GmbH, part of Springer Nature 2021
G. Cisek, *The Triumph of Artificial Intelligence*,
https://doi.org/10.1007/978-3-658-34896-0_7

industry are just more than 3% in wage group 1 with 2398 € and it is only a question of time until this strategy leads to absurdity. The same disproportionality can be seen in the development of the ratio between average income and top salaries. Whereas in the past the boss earned about 10 times as much as the average employee, today it is about 60 times more. There is a quasi-scientific method for "fair" pay determination by means of job evaluation. According to the HAY job value profile method, which is used by 80% of the world's largest companies according to Fortune 500 to determine their income classes, the average job value in Germany is 356 points. The highest job value of the top positions in the German economy is probably around 33,000 points. The Federal Statistical Office gives an average annual income of around 47,000 € for 2018. Then it only takes a simple rule of three to show all annual salaries above 4.5 million euros as "naughty". To the top manager for whom this salary is too little, the aged author would reply that he has not yet encountered an "irreplaceable person" in his personnel management consulting work. This ethical limit I have postulated does not, of course, apply to managing entrepreneurs who bear the capital risk, like Wiedekind in his day, who invested millions of his own in Porsche AG in order to modernize it successfully.

But these are all minimal effects gnawing away at our social system compared to the disruptive cuts AI will cause in the foreseeable future. Whether the goal of "full unemploy-ment," as envisioned by Arthur C. Clarke,[2] will be achieved with AI is very much in doubt, but that it will soon probably snatch away jobs worldwide is more than likely. However, when the McKinsey consultancy, Jerry Kaplan, Carl Frey and Toby Walsh quote the figure of 47%, or at the World Economic Forum 2017 there was talk of only 48% of working hours being performed by humans in 2020, this is surely just gimmicky pseudo-accuracy or simply demonstrably false.[3] Given the dynamics of AI innovation, no one can really seriously predict how many and which jobs will actually be eliminated over the next 20 years. And which profession will become extinct because of AI is not yet clear either. That garbage collectors, policemen and plumbers will keep their jobs, as Michio Kaku claims,[4] may be true, as perhaps Erik Brynjolfsson's hopeful view of engineers, or Manuela Lenzen's opinion of children's educators being safe.[5] But when it comes to the supposedly safe jobs for nurses, gardeners, cooks or receptionists, major doubts are justified. Even the creative types like critical journalists, whom Kaku does not see in danger, should not be so sure. If so far the pen has been stronger than the sword, soon it will be the chip, not the human.[6] Eberl is also mistaken if he believes that master craftsmen in the automotive

---

[2] Arthur C. Clark: "The goal of the future is full unemployment, so we can play." In: "Los Angeles Free Press" interview, (pp. 42–43, 47), April 25, 1969.

[3] See Jerry Kaplan, op. cit. p. 136; Toby Walsh, op. cit. p. 118; Walter Simon, op. cit. p. 147; Andrea Cornelius, op. cit. p. 113.

[4] See Michio Kaku, Physics of the future, Inventions that will transform our lives, p. 305.

[5] See Manuela Lenzen, op. cit. p. 200.

[6] See Michio Kaku, op. cit., p. 307 and p. 339.

industry have their "gut feeling" to secure their jobs. The author has experienced the amusing scene where such a master craftsman was presented with an AI-pressed car roof for inspection and smugly found three minimal damage spots, but lost his smile when it was proven to him that with the previous production technology about 300 such almost invisible defects had escaped his "gut feeling".[7]

However, AI will not only destroy the jobs that are taken over by robots through "deskilling" of operational functions,[8] but also create new ones. According to Wolfgang Wahlster, there is already a shortage of more than 5000 computer scientists in Germany,[9] and Boston Consulting concludes that although around 600,000 jobs will be lost by 2025, one million new ones will be created.[10] These include such new jobs as "behavioral pychologist," "user interface designer," "customer experience researcher," or "digital consultant" for design thinking and minimum viable products* (MVPs).[11] Data Scientists, the Chief Digital Officer (CDO), the Chief Technology Officer (CTO), or the Chief Artificial Intelligence Officer (CAIO)[12] or the "Algorithmicists"[13] take care of the digital transformation of the company. In the hospital, the "Medical Empathy Officer" will soon step up to support the Dr. AIG*.[14] And in construction, the BIM (Building Information Modeling) Manager is already becoming increasingly popular.[15]

AI will also further spread the new forms of work related to "crowdwork"or "crowd sourcing".[16]

When companies pursue the strategy "fail fast, fail cheap", the "Scrum" method is often used, because here the project is divided into intervals, which are processed by Scrum teams in sprints with great time discipline. Here, the Scrum master also sometimes uses external specialists in the crowd for "swarming" or "mob programming".[17] But these are atypical, privileged crowdworkers. The central category of crowdwork is called

---

[7] See Ulrich Eberl, op. cit. p. 236.

[8] See Jerry Kaplan, op. cit. p. 132.

[9] See Peter Buxmann/Holger Schmidt, op. cit. p. 28.

[10] See Ulrich Eberl, op. cit. p. 245.

[11] * https://de.wikipedia.org/wiki/Minimum_Viable_Product: A Minimum Viable Product (MVP), literally a "minimally viable product," is the first minimally functional iteration of a product that must be developed to meet customer, market, or functional needs with minimal effort and ensure actionable feedback.
See Bettina Volkens/Kai Anderson, Digital Human, Der Mensch im Mittelpunkt der Digitalisierung, Frankfurt a. M., 2018, p. 185.

[12] Peter Gensch, op. cit., p. 78 ff.

[13] Viktor Mayer-Schönberger/Kenneth Cukier, op. cit. p. 226.

[14] Christian Maté, op. cit., p. 131.
*AIG = Artificial Intelligence General.

[15] See https://www.ingenieur.de/karriere/arbeitsleben/alltag/wie-wird-man-bim-manager/

[16] See Johannes Wärter, Crowdwork, Vienna, 2019 pp. 19 ff.

[17] See Boris Gloger, Scrum Think Big, Munich, 2017, p. 31.

"microtasking", sometimes also "cognitive piecework". The term "cognitive piecework," or mental piecework, was coined by crowdsourcing researcher Irani. The category microtasking describes the performance of microtasks for micro amounts of money. Morozov calls it more cynically "digitally divided slave labor," and Amazon's "Mechanical Turks" platform places freelancers with companies. Lenzen rightly states that the "clickworkers"or "task rabbits"who are assigned by Leah Busque on his mini-job marketplace as "tasker members" within the framework of the gig economy for everyday tasks such as cleaning, moving, transporting and manual tasks belong to the precariously employed, but still find work with these placement platforms.[18]

But one must fear with Walsh that the losers will be the 20–30 year old men without a school-leaving certificate, whose earned income will be below the subsistence level.[19] The AI will therefore probably force the "unconditional basic income", which is increasingly being discussed, as a solution for the "social fallow". In the meantime there are already enough proposals for the financing of this transfer. Bill Gates, as one of the profiteers of AI, has proposed the introduction of a robot tax, which leads Lenzen to propose a tax on algorithms as well.[20] And Eberl brings an "automation dividend" into play, which should feed the unconditional basic income as a company levy.[21] In this way, "Pigou taxes"[22] could also be introduced for AI-induced "social damage". Swedish philosopher Nick Bostrum confidently assumes that AI-driven explosive growth could provide for "all unemployed citizens quite easily."[23]

With such security of supply, it is to be feared that the most bizarre skills will come to light to supplement the basic income. Brewing beer or other swill, making hand pottery or cheese, as Walsh advises,[24] is baloney and long out of fashion. How about hand-knit car seat covers or hand-scored glass for posh mansions? Beware Kaplan's recommendation to sell poetry "versed" by oneself to the rich![25] The so-called "kohlrabi apostles" from Monte Verità above Ascona already had very bad experiences with this in the 1920s. And with Hermann Hesse, Ernst Bloch or Gerhard Hauptmann, they were certainly no literary dilettantes. Nevertheless, the Ticinese country folk refused monetary redemption of the

---

[18] See Manuela Lenzen, op. cit. p. 203.

[19] See Toby Walsh, op. cit., p. 134; Slavoj Žižek, Hegel im verdrahteten Gehirn, Frankfurt a. M., 2020, p. 41.

[20] See Manula Lenzen, op. cit. p. 207.

[21] See Ulrich Eberl, op. cit. p. 242.

[22] https://de.wikipedia.org/wiki/Pigou-Steuer: "A Pigou tax is a specific case of incentive taxes, that is, taxes that have less of a fiscal purpose and more of a purpose primarily to direct behavior. It is named after Arthur Cecil Pigou."

[23] Nick Bostrum, Superintelligence, Scenarios of a Coming Revolution, Translated from English by Jan-Erik Strasser, 1st edition, Berlin, 2014, p. 229.

[24] See Toby Walsh, op. cit. p. 144.

[25] See Jerry Kaplan, op. cit. p. 149.

poetry slips offered and only pityingly gave the early "alternatives" gabbage and other vegetables.

7.2   Is the Faculty to Speak Turning Yellow?: The Asocial "Social Media"

Every day, more is typed worldwide than has been written down in the past history of mankind with the most diverse characters. The only comforting thing is that at least the trees are spared for the most part, because the writing is done digitally.

If a news service provides you with 140 characters (in the meantime "generously" extended to 280 characters) for expressing your opinion, then it proves that you are either only trusted with limited argumentation skills or qualified views are not of interest, but the statements are only of importance for the "customer profile". If you look at some Twitter notes or comments on the online articles of even sophisticated providers, you get the impression that upper and lower case letters, punctuation rules and the grammatical rulebook have been suspended in the meantime.

In the language of the youth at least funny word innovations like "Buttergolem" or "Gönnjamin"(indulge yourself) are still visible, but mostly only language brutalization is to be lamented. If in Franconian it is traditionally not "der Einzige" (the only one) but "der Einzigste" (the most only one), that still has dialectal charm. But when journalists and high-ranking politicians have "no trouble at all" in "superlativizing" the word "none" and semi-humanists "upimpose" some things where optrude or simply "imposing" would have sufficed, one need not be surprised that hardly anyone notices anymore that he actually means "homology" when he speaks of "analogies". But when the German Academy for Language and Poetry conjures up the earth-shaking transformation of the "aufwendig" (elaborate) into the "aufwändig" (elaborate) with artful effort, instead of finally abolishing the umlauts and the sharp "ß" that are unspeakable for international keyboards, one cannot hope for any help from there in the fight against rampant speechlessness.

Talking is replaced by chatting with the accompanying loss of social presence.[26] This is most obvious when a young couple sits in a bar and, instead of smiling at each other and murmuring something pleasant, confirms the mostly predefined word phrases on their smartphones at an admirable speed. Sociologist Sherry Turkle therefore very aptly calls her new bestseller "Alone together".[27] The smartphone is thus becoming the "control center of life"[28] in the Internet age, and the "secularization of communication"[29] is thus advancing. What Morozov means by this becomes clear again when one reads the

---

[26] See Bettina Volkens/Kai Anderson, op. cit. p. 78.

[27] Sherry Turkle, Alone together, London, 2017.

[28] Malte-Christian Gruber/Jochen Bung/Sascha Ziemann, op. cit. p. 137.

[29] Evegeny Morozov, op. cit. p. 112.

correspondence of, for example, the Privy Councillor Goethe or Richard Wagner, with their linguistic sensitivity and conspicuous structural skill.

If the stylistic inferiority of social media were still bearable for those who are largely insensitive to language, the content of the scraps of words is truly unacceptably antisocial. When even hardened politicians are emotionally affected by this and feel compelled to sue against it, the term "social media"takes on a cynical, stale aftertaste.

If you then witness how these media filter out negativity as much as possible, or how the "memification of public life" is geared towards "hyping up" news that is perhaps irrelevant in terms of content so that it becomes as much of an online hit as possible,[30] you quickly lose trust in the information services. However, this cannot be blamed on AI; in this context, AI has to take care of translation robots and the turn-taking (language change) problem*, so that the global citizenry can communicate with each other without interference.

7.3 Are We Becoming a Real World Community?: The Ubiquity of the "Homeland"

As these lines are being written, the Corona virus (SARS-CoV-2) is raging worldwide. There is no sign of a global strategy to combat it. Instead, the self-interests of the nation states are being defended, in some cases with more than ruthless methods. Has globalisation thus outlived its usefulness?—Not at all, for it is not politics but economics that has primacy and will continue to pursue it stringently in the sense of a world economic community.

Two opposing currents will be observed. The global economic interconnections and interdependencies will intensify and thus a fundamental cultural standardization will be unavoidable, if only because of the globally standardized consumption and service offers. At the same time, however, regional and local consciousness will increasingly resist this standardization.

This phenomenon could already be observed in the so-called developing countries in the 1970s. At that time, the term "indigenization" was coined for it, a form of cultural change in which traditional societies superficially adopt something foreign, but then integrate it into their traditional culture as something culturally adaptive of their own. The Indonesian "Teh Botol" is a successful example of this. In an Indonesian household, there is always lukewarm tea from the local tea plantations. Nevertheless, the company Sosro has dared to market this tea, heavily sweetened, as a cold drink in cola-like bottles. In Indonesia—after all, a domestic market with over 260 million potential customers—this bottle has long

---

[30] See Evegeny Morozov, op. cit. p. 266 ff.

https://de.wikipedia.org/wiki/Sprecherwechsel: "Turn taking is a common phenomenon in conversations that ensures that and how several turns are distributed among the participants in the conversation.

been the best-selling beverage and is now even sold worldwide. Another example are the Javanese kretek cigarettes. Dried clove powder is added to the Indonesian tobacco for this purpose, resulting not only in a pleasantly seductive drug scent, but also in many a burn spot when the powder sparks. Although these handmade, cone-shaped pleasure sticks are more expensive than the imported brands, they are preferred by the countrymen.

Comparable tendencies of "regionalisation" can also be observed here. The now gradually withering '68 generation can be seen smiling mildly at the hot desire of young families for an allotment garden, the sedimented "grounding" of the philistine bourgeoisie in order to assure themselves of healthy self-sufficiency. Back then, like the author in Berkeley, we tore up asphalted streets to convert them into "people's parks" with tomato plants. But not for food security, but to protest the sealing of the glorious California landscape! And local "homegrown" is now all the rage, even in better circles. Among the author's—admittedly privileged—social partners, there are so many varieties of "home-shot, home-brewed and home-cooked" in the C2C trade that the trade supervisory authorities should be terrified. This illustrated the more sympathetic side of cultural or native identification. The dangerously malevolent alternative of global division can be seen, for example, with the terrorist Boko Haram ("Westernization Is Sacrilege") movement, which, while striving for globalization in the sense of pan-Islamism, is irreconcilably opposed to other social value scales, even if it is happy to make use of AI-technological possibilities.

But against the economically conformist "world home", even it has no chance. AI knows no boundaries! And it also offers many pleasant things in everyday life. In the past, a short call from Jakarta to Cologne cost around DM 100, the airmail edition of the FAZ (Frankfurter Allgemeine Zeitung) reached Jakarta with a 14-day delay, and today you can read its online version worldwide in "real time". And you can not only chat for free with your loved ones scattered around the globe, you can even see them doing it, although this does not always turn out to be an advantage for social interaction. The shopping experience has also come to feel "at home" wherever you go. Whether you're shopping at Walmart, Carrefour, and Ikea in Taipei or Washington D.C., you're "at home." The customer journey and merchandise planning are always the same: First come the special offers with perishable or expiring goods, the refrigerated goods are found energy-saving in the sunlight-less part of the salesroom, and just before the checkout, the "grouching items" that clamoring children pester; for "compelling" goods of daily use such as pet food, one has to bend down to the lowest shelves, while optional consumer items are seductively emblazoned on the "line of sight," and the meat counters are appetizingly freshened up globally with the same artificial light.—Even going out in the evening makes the global citizen feel at home. Whether in the steakhouse Maredo, at Starbucks or Trade's Vic—you take no risks, because the range of goods in Dubai does not differ in the least from that in Munich. Wrong!—for collectors, Starbucks occasionally stocks its stores with local landmark-printed mugs.—"What does all this have to do with AI?" you ask. But of course, sophisticated software controls the inventory management system in these chains. You might well call this standardization "digital culture."[31]

While nation states are still considering the political possibilities of AI in terms of "open government"[32] to encourage their citizens and the business community to participate more directly, digital platforms and app stores such as Ebay, Amazon or Baidu have long spanned the globe without borders and without regard for any national telecommunications rights.[33]

Imagine self-proclaimed and -pleasing "influencers"taking up the idea of "digital government" and attempting homeless digital world politics. Then Morozov's term "Liquid Democracy"[34] takes on a dramatic and highly dangerous twist of meaning. This may hopefully remain an unfounded concern. But that the above-mentioned oligarchic platforms will increasingly dominate the world by way of an "algocracy", as Eberl vividly describes this development,[35] seems inevitable.

The last chapter of this book will deal with the concomitants of these lines of development.

---

[31] Bettina Volkens/Kai Anderson, op. cit. p. 151.

[32] See Evegeny Morozov, op. cit. p. 165 ff.

[33] See https://www.bmwi.de/Redaktion/DE/Artikel/Digitale-Welt/digitale-plattformen.html

[34] See Evegeny Morozov, op. cit. p. 184 ff.

[35] Ulrich Eberl, op. cit., p. 274.

Paradise Times or the End of the World?: The Future with AI

8

Futurology is the art of scratching before it itches.
Robert Jungk

Many a clever head has been embarrassingly wrong with predictions about the future. But some things have also worked out quite well. There have been discoveries that have come about more quickly than predicted, such as the breakdown of DNA,[1] but also innovations that will come about later than predicted, such as self-driving traffic, which would already be technically possible in terms of vehicles, but for which the necessary infrastructure is still lacking in large parts.

The author of this book is also aware of the risk of being wrong about the future of our AI-soaked lives. But nevertheless, he is driven by the desire to approach this topic in a very imaginary way and to speculate about it freely in the last three sections of this chapter.

But first there are very brittle legal and security issues to discuss in relation to AI.

8.1 Guilt and Atonement?: Legal Aspects of AI

Back in the days when the use of a mobile phone, due to its bulky size and weight, was equivalent to weight training, the author sat in an old tram that still derived its kinetic energy from a sparking overhead line. When the short conversation (at that time there was no flat rate, the charges would have been more like a "fat rate") was over, a lady from the bench opposite grumbled at him: "But you know that your mobile phone is not good for our

---

[1] See, among others, Ray Kurzweil, op. cit. p. 251.

© Springer Fachmedien Wiesbaden GmbH, part of Springer Nature 2021
G. Cisek, *The Triumph of Artificial Intelligence*,
https://doi.org/10.1007/978-3-658-34896-0_8

brain!" and looked indignantly at him and then worryingly at her child. The output of the author's spontaneous "virtual" replica, "Madam, there is hardly much damage to your brain." was happily denied by his neocortex because of its early childhood socialization to politeness. But in this encounter, the hostility to technology in Germany had been brought home to him again. There we were jerking unhesitatingly through the beautiful old town under about 500 V of voltage and the child mother was worrying about the cell phone because of its about 5 V. And she worried with many of her compatriots for a long time, while in Asia the trend to the second mobile phone became already visible.

What a difference between the "Zeitgeist" (spirit of the age) of Silicon Valley and the "Deutschangst"! We may have had a finely honed Basic Data Protection Regulation (DSGVO) since 1995, which has caused many a village association to give up because of the many requirements, but we still have a long way to go before we have a 5G (fifth generation of mobil service) network that would make truly voluminous data traffic possible in the first place.

The AI aversion is also present in the European Parliament. There, MEPs are demanding that ADM processes (ADM = Automated Decision Making) be made "explainable" and be cross-checked by humans and overruled if necessary.[2] For the concerned, it should be pointed out that the research direction XAI (Explainable AI) is now dealing with this problem.[3]

Imagine, if this is done again by "experts", who cannot distinguish "Kobold" from "Cobalt" without renouncing a judgement about car batteries. Because experts know that when using neural networks the solution process often cannot be traced back, they recommend in all seriousness, for example, "to leave an approved medical device that uses neural networks in its well-trained original state".[4] Translated into technical reality, this means: "The device is prohibited from further machine learning! With such a basic attitude, Europe should "establish itself as a data power beyond the USA and China".[5] To this, the European Commission President declares with breathtaking arrogance: "Europe leads in AI",[6] whereas at the same time the Süddeutsche Zeitung reported that China had overtaken the USA for the first time in 2019 with 59,000 patent applications, while Germany and the Netherlands saw a decline in applications."[7] The Tagesspiegel wrote about a study by the World Intellectual Property Organization (WIPO): "Among the 500 most active applicants for AI patents—both companies and research institutions—

---

[2] See Stefan Krempl, EU MEPs call for "explainable" and transparent artificial intelligence, in: Heise Online, 23.01.2020.

[3] See, among others, Marion Herger, Wenn Affen von Affen lernen, Wie künstliche Intelligenz uns erst richtig zum Menschen macht, Kulmbach 2020, p. 253.

[4] See Peter Hanke, Bei KI-Risiken besser besser nicht nur die EU fragen, in: NetApp, Trending Topics, 2 March 2020.

[5] See Stefan Krempl, op. cit.

[6] Ibid.

[7] China ahead worldwide, in: Süddeutsche Zeitung, 7 April 2020.

were 110 Chinese universities, 20 from the US and 19 from South Korea. Only four were from Europe."[8]

Allegedly, techno-pioneers are praising the European General Data Protection Regulation as "groundbreaking".[9] The Federation of German Industries (BDI), however, warns against over-regulation of AI and states that no IT application is known that is not already sufficiently regulated by existing law.[10]

As long as we are still dealing with "weak" AI without a will and consciousness of its own, it is probably not possible to hold it criminally responsible, but at best its creator or user.[11] In the case of civil claims, Kaplan believes that corporate law should cover the rights and obligations of intelligent machines.[12] But will this still apply if the supervisory boards of the future are made up of circuits,[13] as Brockmann suspects?—This unanswered question makes it clear that specific legal issues and ethics problems do indeed arise for AI, some of which are raised below.

For example, the "intellectual property" or copyright for AI developments needs to be clarified. The German Patent and Trade Mark Office (DPMA) states: "Artificial intelligence methods are mostly mathematical solutions implemented in software, i.e. computer-implemented methods. These are only accessible to patent protection to a limited extent, since computer programs are not patentable per se." In Eckhardt's view, according to the German reading, existing property rights do not protect ideas and concepts, but only their realization. The best protection, he recommends, is secrecy. At the very least, the risk of plagiarism must be addressed through contractual non-disclosure agreements.[14] This coincides with the author's experience that many a company hesitates to even apply for a patent for innovations in order "not to wake any sleeping dogs".

This leads to the fundamental question of who has sovereignty over the proliferating bevy of data that AI is sparking. Is my own data cloud mine to claim for or prohibit the use of? The answer directs us to the problem of how to balance common welfare against individual interest. A digital medical record for everyone would be of great benefit in caring for and protecting public health, but not only doctors but also some "libertarian" citizens resist its introduction. Some scientists would recommend that he sell his health data to the state or other interested parties.[15] Daytum founder Nick Feiton, however, would

---

[8] Artificial intelligence: number of AI patents rises sharply, in: Tagesspiegel, 31 Jan. 2019.

[9] Stefan Krempl, op. cit.

[10] See BDI warns EU Commission against overregulation of AI, in: wirtschaft.com of 16 Feb. 2020.

[11] See, among others, Brion Knutson, The Robot with ulterior motives, in: John Brockmann, op. cit., p. 206; Kurt Gray, Killer thinking machines keep our conscience clear, in: John Brockmann, op. cit., p. 371.

[12] See Jerry Kaplan, op. cit. p. 121.

[13] Martin Rees, Organic intelligence has no long-term future, in: John Brockmann, op. cit. p. 52.

[14] Jens Eckhardt, Industrie 4.0—Rechtliche Aspekte, in: Christiana Köhler-Schute, loc. cit.

[15] See Viktor Mayer-Schönberger/Kenneth Cukier, op. cit. p. 185.

counter: "If you want privacy, you have to pay for it."[16] It is to be expected that the "data donors" will increasingly demand acknowledgement for the use of their "digits" once they become aware of the data value.

Another problem area is the use of robot lawyers. With LegTech or DoNotPay, they are already active in many ways in the USA. But in our country, for example, Katharina Zweig worries that the algorithms used for this purpose discriminate on the basis of race.[17] This may be provable, but then this can also be corrected. This is likely to be much more difficult to remedy in the case of racist judges, who certainly exist. One study showed that judges in Israel were significantly milder in their sentences immediately after a break with refreshments.[18] And certainly one could list numerous other examples of how judicial justice is human with however much "tact." The author rather prefers tactless robo-judges, to whom I can prove misjudgments much more objectively.

The author is also constantly amazed at the intensity with which this algorithm ethics is always discussed anew in the question of guilt and the problem of weighing up accidents involving self-driving cars. The conflict is constantly presented when the vehicle causes an unavoidable accident in order to demonstrate the immorality of autonomous vehicles. According to which ethical criteria should the algorithm decide?

Should he decide according to the sum of the lives saved or according to the "quality" of the persons concerned or according to what other criteria? The author is keen to start by stating with relish that AI makes such a consideration possible in the first place. A human driver would have run over the group of people long before he would have sorted out the conflict of interest. Any decision made by the algorithm is therefore more rational than that of a human driver.

Whether, in the above case, the algorithm steers the vehicle into a group of senior citizens in order to save a baby in a pram or vice versa can be regulated precisely from a technical point of view, but is admittedly difficult to weigh up ethically and certainly depends on society's scale of values.

The ethical decision itself, however, would probably be quite easy to program in a culturally specific way. Thus, the decision will be different in a social system that reveres old age than in a social community that indulges in youthfulness. In Japan and other Far Eastern cultures, priority would probably be given to the old, while other civilizations might want to save the young.

Interesting in this context are the results of a study by MIT. In an extensive survey on this problem in different cultural circles, the following results emerged: In Japan—as suspected—the majority would let older people survive, the French would charmingly give preference to women in accidents, and for Germany the results show the technology

---

[16] See Evegeny Morozov, op. cit. p. 392.

[17] See Katharina Zweig, op. cit. p. 212 ff.

[18] See Marion Herger, op. cit. p. 152.

aversion typical for us and also still fueled by the media, in that the majority of respondents want to leave accident behavior to chance and not to a rational algorithm.

Udo di Fabio, former constitutional judge and chairman of the European Ethics Commission, has commented on this so-called trolley dilemma: "Who should be given priority to be run down? Every human life is equal. To say that in our constitutional order is almost trivial. But it also leads to the fact that selection according to characteristics, according to man, woman or age, is inadmissible." In this respect, Precht does not need to invoke theatrically: "Death algorithms must never exist."[19] For our cultural sphere it is legally ruled out and other societies should be allowed their own judgment.

According to the German Ethics Commission, too, "any qualification according to personal characteristics (age, gender, physical or mental constitution) is strictly prohibited in unavoidable accident situations." But this commission has fundamental reservations about autonomous driving anyway: "A complete networking and central control of all vehicles in the context of a digital traffic infrastructure is ethically questionable if and to the extent that it cannot safely exclude risks of total monitoring of road users and manipulation of vehicle control."[20]

It is not known to the author what the Commission's position is on the more than 3000 traffic deaths caused annually by non-AI controlled traffic in Germany alone.

Before we get to more futuristic legal problems below, for the sake of completeness, let's mention Asimov's three robot laws, according to which a robot

1. Not to harm or injure any human being,
2. Must obey human orders (as far as this contradicts not the first law) and
3. Shall protect its own existence to the extent that this does not conflict with Law 1 and/or 2.

So far, except in science fiction novels, you haven't heard of robots self-destructing, not following the programming by humans, or knowingly violating them—so why these silly laws are constantly cited remains a mystery.[21] They're not needed for weak AI, and strong AI won't care! Simon rightly lists the ethical demands on intelligent systems such as "peaceful coexistence", "helping people in need" or "diversity, non-discrimination and fairness" rather smilingly, only to state laconically that "the main AI players from the American West Coast and the digital mandarins from China are unlikely to get into the ethics boat".[22]

---

[19] Richard David Precht, op. cit. p. 192.

[20] Ibid.

[21] See inter alia Erik Brynjolfsson/Andrew McAfee, op. cit. p. 39; Brian Knutson, The robot with ulterior motives, in: John Brock-Mann, op. cit, p. 208; Manuela Lenzen, op. cit. p. 142; Ulrich Eberl, op. cit. p. 307; Gernot Bauer, op. cit. p. 15; Toby Walsh, op. cit. p. 105; Walter Simon, op. cit. p. 223 f.

[22] See Walter Simon, op. cit. p. 240.

Fig. 8.1 FPV video goggles
(Source: Cinemizer Oled)

The liability issue for damage caused by AI-driven machines has already been briefly addressed above. But it is interesting to consider whether computers can already claim "machine rights". According to Günther, who feels that today's civil law is outdated, there is nothing to be said against granting technical artefacts subjective legal protection or partial legal capacity.[23] Lierfeld, too, considers it justifiable to grant rights to our "mind children", provided they are able to develop individual experiences (qualia) and reflection. In September 2003, Martine Rosenblatt even brought in vain a fictitious case before the International Bar Association on behalf of the fictitious BINA 48, which had allegedly already attained consciousness because it could calculate faster than the human brain, in order to sue for injunctive relief against its shutdown. One may well justifiably dismiss this performance as a premature marketing campaign for Ms. Rosenblatt's law firm, because until "strong" AI will bring machine legal personalities to fruition, lawyers for these problems can keep their hands in their laps for a while longer.

But now we want to take a look into this promising future.

8.2   Virtual or Real?: New Forms of Life

Volland correctly states that " representational technology via goggles or headset has now reached the point" where "no significant differences between reality and virtuality are discernible to our sensory organs."[24] Indeed, today "virtual reality" (VR), as Damien Broderick first called "the representation and simultaneous perception of reality and its physical properties in a real-time computer-generated, interactive virtual environment" in his 1982 novel *The Judas Mandala,* has advanced to the point where it not only deceptively pixelates reality, but can even render it more "surreal" in the truest sense of the word with augmented reality (AR) effects. For a convincing immersion, in addition to the head-mounted display (HMD), FPV glasses (first-person view glasses, see Fig. 8.1) are now

---

[23] See Jan-Philpp Günther, Embodied Robots—Time for a Legal Reassessment?, in: Christiana Köhler-Schute, loc. cit.

[24] Holger Volland, op. cit. p. 186.

available, with which one can experience car races from the "pole position", or AR glasses (data glasses), which project Internet pages or holograms onto the field of vision.

A virtual reality headset whose sensors also detect head movements, a 3D mouse, a flystick to simulate movement and the data glove for haptic simulations can become so exhaustingly "real" that they can occasionally lead to simulator sickness. On a positive note, however, VR has also been used successfully therapeutically to reduce anxiety or pain. Paraplegics can use it to jog virtually and, amazingly, show psychosomatic reactions as if they had really been running, and space travelers are reported to use VR productions from time to time to escape the confines of the space capsule.

The virtual experience becomes even more intense when a three-dimensional "Cave Automatic Virtual Environment" (CAVE = cave with automated, virtual environment) is available and one can experience virtual worlds together with others. In the author's experience, when such a "cave cube" with 3D-capable Light Emitting Diodes (LED) walls or Liquid Cristal (LC) displays uses its six projection surfaces, one can quickly miss one's sense of balance.

However, it must be admitted that today the CAVE is used more for scientific and industrial purposes. In the medical field, for example, it can be used to display organs or visualize enzymes. Engineers use it to work teletechnically on virtual constructions, just as CAD designers use it to walk through their models in a three-dimensional panorama system.

So, in summary, we can state that VR and AR technology already offers all the possibilities to immerse oneself in artificial worlds without any restrictions. It is therefore to be regretted that the entertainment and leisure industry, despite these fantastic technical possibilities, hardly knows how to offer anything apart from the rather redundant war and racing games.

After all, in its study on megatrends 2014 for the "home sphere", the Zukunftsinstitut (Institute for future) sees opportunities for virtual holidays.

The offers described therein for "interactive travelling" without having to step outside the front door of one's own home[25] still seem rather conservative, even if they are in line with "political correctness" in the sign of the environmental crisis. But if the real holiday trip is only replaced by a virtually identical excursion, the great possibilities of VR technology are gambled away. Gimmicks such as digital tour guides or "secret doors" that allow you to discover little-known places are probably not enough to really keep you away from the physically real trip. You can also do that analogue with good travel guides and a little bit of your own imagination.

The added value must lie in the fact that one can experience on the virtual journey what is not possible in reality, e.g. sailing on a felucca to the rock temple at Abu Simbel (actually: Ipsambul) on a virtual holiday on the Nile to discuss with Ramses II about his

---

[25] Janine Seitz, Christian Schuldt, Christian Rauch, Anjy Kirig, Cornelia Kelber, Thomas Huber, Jana Ehret, Mikrotrends 2014 Technologie Spezial, in: Kulturinstitut vom Februar 2014.

mysterious royal wife Nefertari. To sweat under the mask as a barong or rangda dancer on a digital Bali vacation to the demonic sound of the gamelan orchestra would be an experience no tour operator, no matter how intellectualized, can offer. For those who prefer a more natural experience, there is no better way to enjoy the splendour of the flowers than to be a bee in Holland's tulip fields. How about a virtual wine tasting? You put the virtual reality headset over your head—comfortably lounging in the living room chair - after having placed the tongue shoe before, beam yourself into the beautiful garden of an idyllic Bordeaux chateau and virtually pour a 16er Chateau Clinet Pomerol or even a Château Petrus from 2009 behind your cartilage. The supposed life-prolonging effects of resveratrol are unfortunately not guaranteed in digital red wine, and the tongue shoe admittedly still needs a bit of a technical upgrade. But the virtual "diet feast" is near!

These examples seem too abstruse to you? There are people who get themselves locked up in an "Escape Room" for a lot of money, in order to then escape their imprisonment with a lot of effort—so there are also analogous strange pleasure addictions. In Cologne they say with mild wisdom: "Jeder Jeck is anders" (Each crazy is different).

With the above examples, the author only wants to show what exotic-bizarre possibilities of virtual forms of experience we would have at our disposal. Much more down-to-earth applications in industrial training operations have long been commonplace. Virtual concerts and sporting events have not only been realized since the Corona crisis, and in the medical field AI is already at work in virtual patient rooms via robotic nurses.

The latter leads us to a VR target group whose need is paired with equivalent purchasing power: the fastest-growing cohorts in the population pyramid, the 90- and 100-year-old. They usually suffer from limited physical mobility. Developing special virtual experience programs for them must of course go hand in hand with application training for the corresponding media and devices. The computer courses that the "silversurfers" like to attend (the author recently had to repeat his cheerful "Internet training course "The Mouse Doesn't Bite" for participants older than 80 twice because of great demand) show that the "old people" certainly have a great inclination for this. Such VR/AR offers meet exactly the needs of the ageing population, who, with increasing life expectancy, are approaching the new way of life of "cocooning", i.e. "withdrawing into private domestic life", nolens volens due to health reasons. And it is not only the elderly for whom "active cocooning"makes life easier. Other social groups tend towards this way of life for a variety of reasons. Bavarian Radio had this to say about it: "Faith Popcorn, who is often called the mother of trend research, tracked down this trend in 1981 and named it "cocooning." "Cocooning" describes the retreat into one's own four walls, the trend towards bunking down together with home service. People who have found the outside world too complicated, stressful and uninteresting withdraw into their own small, manageable circle of life as if into a cocoon.

Overall, "cocooning" channels many trend currents: It represents people's dwindling desire to explore new territory, as well as the shrinking of one's horizons of

Fig. 8.2 Wormhole (Source: shutterstock Wormhole)

responsibility and a certain indifference that is rampant in a highly individualized society."[26]

Cocooning is not yet a "disembodiment", but it is already a "quasi-desocialization" and at least a signal of strangely alien social developments. The next section will speculate on even more futurological trends.

8.3 "Disembodiment" of the Human Being?: Optimization of Human Functionality

To make it clear right away: We are not going to ride the space elevator into the "beyond" at the carbon pillar here, or say goodbye with Haku on a wormhole (see Fig. 8.2) into the universe,[27] nor indulge in interstellar sex, as Hillenbrand coyly hints at in his new thriller, "Qube."[28]

Here, we "only" want to frame scenarios that optimize the "human construct" even with "weak AI" in the coming decades, whereby "optimize" implies a valuation that can, of

---

[26] BR-online, "Cocooning", broadcast from 23.11.2010.

[27] See Michio Haku, op. cit., p. 408 ff.

[28] See Tom Hillenbrand, QUBE, Cologne, 2020, p. 396 ff.

course, be questioned. At the same time, we must be aware that the visionary innovations highlighted below are likely to follow the same pattern that most developments have experienced: After the "innovation trigger" and the associated "peak of inflated expectations" with exaggerated expectations, the valley of disappointments ("trough of disillusionment") follows until the technology successfully settles on the path of enlightenment ("slope of enlightenment") with many a clever input and experience.[29]

We take the liberty in this section not to go beyond the first step, but to get excited about the chances of physical "expansion" without setting ourselves ideological or ethical limits.

The most obvious—because it is already successfully underway—is probably that we will first use "human digitalization" to compensate or even overcompensate for our physical inadequacies through AI applications. It has already begun with prosthetic limbs, and so will organic transhumanism creep.[30] AI proteomics will push us to "superhuman" physical feats, so we can expect a cyborg Olympics where "transatletes" will jump house-high and -far and run as fast as panthers or far longer than today's ultrarunners. It would actually be a pleasurable challenge for architects to design cyborg stadiums with aisles for the throwing disciplines through which javelins and hammers can buzz out for miles. But probably the idea of such a stadium is already anachronistic, because spectators will only want to admire these competitive athletes virtually from their living boxes. If the biological expansion of the body does not succeed via genomics, prosthetics will continue to do so. The "rubber hand illusion", as Metzinger calls the phenomenon proven by brain research with the aid of fMRI (functional magnetic resonance imaging) procedures, helps here, according to which the brain constructs an internalized image of the exoskeletal tool (e.g. the rubber hand) and integrates it into the existing individual body image, so that it gives the user the feeling of "being mine", i.e. feels as if the tool were biologically grown together with his body, which is naturally associated with safe handling of the exoskeleton.[31]

With this epistemic trick of our brain there are now amazing possibilities for the "disembodiment" or better yet: for our "mega-bodiment": For a mountain hike we strap on high carbon stilts, in order to with these "seven-mile-boots" properly "make distance". Of course we don't forget to take the spectral glasses with us, which let us enjoy the sunset with its "marvelous" absorption and emission lines in its chemical composition. The author is what is commonly called a "water rat", although for his physical aesthetics the term "capybara" would be more accurate. And as hard as he tries, snorkels and scuba gear remain very annoying to him. Surely AI should be able to invent more dexterous bodily aids to make a human's sojourn in the depths of the ocean more effortless. If a dog knew of our olfactory limitations, he would laugh at us with his sniffer nose. But he would soon stop

---

[29] See Andreas Syska/Philippe Lievre, op. cit. p. 123.

[30] See Tim O'Reill, What if we are the microbiome of silicon-based AI?, in. John Brockmann, op. cit. p. 267.

[31] See Thomas Metzinger, op. cit. p. 155 ff.

laughing when he learned that the industry is working on "artificial noses" (olfactometers) that can smell not only better but also more accurately than he can and that, in addition to the smell, also provide a chemical analysis of the substance to be sniffed. The still young discipline of "anthrobotics"[32] will certainly make us many an unexpected offer.

The proverb says: "Children can be cruel". The experience of the old ones teaches: "Adults can be at least as horrible." If almost half of the marriages concluded in Germany are divorced, there are probably considerable social deficits in the "human machine". The AI could design training sequences that, after diagnosing the individual deficiencies, improve social behaviour, for example in the sense of conditioning. But perhaps AI, in interdependence with genetic engineering, will find a much more rigorous way for us to maintain emotional relationships completely free of conflict in the future.

For the existence of marriages, this would perhaps be a dubious success, because if AI-based medicine gives us a life expectancy of more than 150 years, the institution of marriage will probably be called into question for some. Since the start of the millennium, life expectancy in our latitudes has already increased by an average of 0.7 years annually. If in the future, wearables constantly monitor our biodata and use it to feed preventive medicine,[33] this factor will improve significantly. If genetic researchers then also eliminate the gene "bcat-1" and other "age genes" using AI technology, life expectancy will increase by another 25% right away, according to scientists from the Swiss Federal Institute of Technology in Zurich (ETH), among others.[34] And who knows what else epigenetics will bring to light to further significantly improve this percentage.

However, the question arises whether we want to merely postpone senescence at all via the path described above. Since 2007, human bladders have been manufactured from biological material with the help of molecular medicine, and since 2009, tracheas. Tissue engineering has long been researching the artificial production of biological tissue for more complex human organs. In this context, Haku speaks confidently of the future "human body shop."[35] Tissue engineering involves taking cells from the donor organism and multiplying them in the laboratory In Vitro (literally, "in a jar"). Many will have the human ear grown on the back of a mouse in mind when reading this (Fig. 8.3).

Meanwhile, the 3D printer makes this more appetizing. In the meantime, it is considered possible that organ cultivation will eventually even be able to reproduce the human brain, or at least activate the growth of sensory cells.

"But then I'm no longer the same", you will certainly hear reproachfully from the sceptics. Well, do these complainers know that they have replaced themselves 100% every 7 years without noticing it?- Every day between 50 and 70 billion cells die in the human

---

[32] Luis de Miranda, op. cit. p. 140.

[33] See Christian Maté, op. cit. p. 79 ff.

[34] See Age gene: How to slow down the aging process, in: Augsburger Allgemeine of December 8, 2015.

[35] Michio Kaku, Physics of the future, op. cit. p. 126.

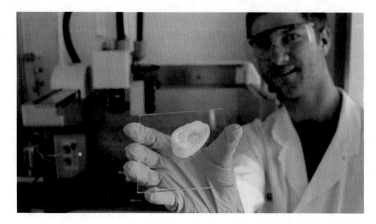

Fig. 8.3 Human ear made from "DNA ink" (Source: Empa Swiss Federal Laboratories for Materials Science and Technology)

body and are replaced, whereby the cell life span varies greatly. White blood cells, for example, are replaced every few hours, while brain cells, on the other hand, are only renewed in decades or not at all, which perhaps explains many a fatal mental outpouring.[36]

The especially brave may not only want to refresh themselves with healthy replacement organs, but experience "disembodiment" as Metzinger describes it in the Ego Tunnel.[37] If it is true that we as "naive realists cannot "experience" the fullness of the complex real world anyway, but that our consciousness is only sufficient for the mastery of a phenomenal self-model (PSM), then it might be interesting to escape one's body in order to experience this reduced fiction of the world in a different physicality.[38]

Not only the "Vites", who spend their lives almost exclusively in the virtual world, will have to dig deep into their pockets for this.[39] Only the privileged will be able to afford the AI services described here. And only if the infrastructure of the place where you live allows it technically at all. The already lamented division of society will therefore manifest itself further, especially if it ends up being not just about virtual pleasures, but about actually "living on". This could lead to a "global caste system" that is not based on cultural or religious ideas, but is purely economic and will lead to dramatic distribution struggles. Perhaps in the end the "Strong AI", which will be the subject of consideration in the last section of this book, will put a surprising end to this tragedy.

---

[36] See Corinne Kroemmer, How many cells die in your body every day?, in: science.lu, November 21, 2013.

[37] See Thomas Metzinger, Der EGO Tunnel, Munich, 2017, p. 116 ff.

[38] See Thomas Metzinger, op. cit., pp. 34 and 116 ff.

[39] See Max Tegmark, op. cit. p. 263.

8.4   Dinosaur Fate?: The Hostile Takeover of the Singularity

Kurzweil is praised for predicting self-driving cars as early as 1986. It didn't take much of a seer to do that, because he could have encountered a bus on the Bundeswehr grounds in Neubieberg as early as the late 1970s, which even then no longer needed the intervention of a driver. Whether his prediction that the "Strong AI", i.e. the "Singularity" would be reached in 2045,[40] will come true is actually of secondary interest. What is more decisive is that almost all experts who deal with AI in technical terms agree in their verdict that it will have come by the end of this century.

Probably there will be no abrupt leap in which this event suddenly manifests itself, but rather a gradual development will lead to this evolutionarily significant occurrence. And humanists and natural scientists will argue about when and whether the monstrous event occurred, because the ASI is also a question of definition.

Thinking, intelligence, consciousness or singularity: all "suitcase" words into which one can pack what anyone wants. Thus Tegmark claims that the advent of thinking machines will be the "most important happening in human history",[41] while in the same book Hidalgo considers thinking machines to be as absurd as thinking humans.[42] So, of course, one can argue that airplanes don't fly, because aerodynamically it's really different from birdie flight, and balloonists don't fly, after all, but "drive." But many a bird would be happy if it could "not fly" like an Airbus.

In the same book, Luca Di Blase derisively considers singularity and transhumanism to be impossible because computers have no cousins and cannot love or urinate.[43] Apart from the fact that the reduction of being human to loving and peeing is outrageously simplistic, Metzinger would reproach him with the fact that the ego tunnel* with its solidified phenomenal self-model denies him a view of the future.[44]

But this is exactly what we want to treat ourselves to now, without bias and in full awareness of its speculative nature.

The driving evolutionary forces will be genomics, nanotechnology, molecular biology and quantum physics, in addition to AI, which is not currently experiencing a winter but rather a midsummer for the time being.

---

[40] See among others Alexander Armbruster, op. cit., p. 46 f.; Eric Brynjolsson/Andrew McCaffee, op. cit., p. 305; Holger Volland, op. cit., p. 146; Jerry Kaplan, op. cit, p. 156 ff; Daniel C. Dennett, The Singularity—A Modern Legend?, in: John Brockmann, op. cit. p. 123; Nick Bostrum, op. cit. p. 16; Michio Kaku, Farewell to the Earth, op. cit. p. 182.

[41] Max Tegmark, Let's Get Ready, in: John Brockmann, op. cit. p. 78.

[42] Cesar Hidalgo, Machines don't think, but neither do people, in: John Brockmann, op. cit. p. 143.

[43] Luca Di Blase, Narratives and Our Culture, in: John Brockmann, op. cit. p. 323.

*Metzinger describes the ego tunnel as an internal construct of the human brain: "Our conscious model of reality is a low-dimensional projection of the unimaginably richer and more substantial physical reality that surrounds us and sustains us."

[44] See Thomas Metzinger, op. cit. p. 47 ff.

They will, as mentioned in the last section, not only make us more functional and life-prolonging, if not immortal, but also drastically change our way of life and our microbiome. True, immortality removes the reproductive obligation of the human species, but until that happens, we will spare the "mothers" the task of carrying offspring for at least the next few decades. Those who can afford it will order their "designer baby" in the " breeding lab" and get the flawless desired child without having to spend 9 months "in other circumstances" for it. We transhumanists will then also usually no longer consume animal flesh or crops, but the 3D printer will serve us a "precious" (let the reader interpret the term entirely for himself) molecular mush according to our biodata and personal aesthetic preferences. The vegan steaks from the 3D printer already exist.[45] And if we notice that the current living landscape does not whet the appetite, the emotional wallpaper or wall displays are changed accordingly and Dynamic Physical Rendering (DPR) is switched on, and by means of the morphing antenna or BCI technology* the "Catome" (claytronic atoms) of the "Gelsenkirchen Baroque" is transformed into an Italian-futuristic designer landscape.[46] Of course, the whole thing also becomes a special haptic experience, because the data suit lets us sublimely feel the different atomic density of the cutlery and the seating furniture. Needless to say, after the nutritionally optimized meal, we indulge in a cocktail of non-addictive designer drugs to stimulate the kick of the virtual trip into orbit a bit.

The real trip to the stars might still involve a certain risk at this point. But we have secured ourselves against this, no—not with travel insurance, but by way of our vitrification,[47] which modern cryonics now makes possible without damage. And besides, as "homo digitalis", we quickly saved our personal singleton[48] in the cloud and on the data stick.

One can easily argue whether humans, transhumans, the AGI (Artificial General Intelligence) or already the embodied ASI (Artificial Super Intelligence) are described here. Probably the onthological gap in[49] between is fluid. In any case, it becomes clear that

---

[45] Eshchar Ben Shitrit, Vegan steak from the 3D printer, in: Spiegel Wissenschaft, 02.07.2020.

[46] *See https://en.wikipedia.org/wiki/Brain-computer_interface: "A brain-computer interface (BCI), sometimes called a neural-control interface (NCI), mind-machine interface (MMI), direct neural interface (DNI), or brain-machine interface (BMI), is a direct communication pathway between an enhanced or wired brain and an external device. BCI differs from neuromodulation in that it provides a bidirectional flow of information. BCIs are often designed to explore, map, assist, augment, or repair human cognitive or sensorimotor functions."
See Michio Kaku, op. cit. p. 176.

[47] https://de.wikipedia.org/wiki/Vitrifizierung: "Vitrification (also called vitrification, from the Latin vitrum 'glass') is the solidification of a liquid by increasing its viscosity while it is cooled—whereby crystallization fails to occur and thus an amorphous material (glass) is formed. This can be achieved, for example, by extremely rapid cooling (e.g. in liquid nitrogen) in conjunction with additives that prevent crystallization (so-called cryoprotectants)."

[48] See, among others, Nick Bostrum, op. cit. p. 160; Thomas Ramge, op. cit. p. 83; Walter Simon, op. cit. p. 217.

[49] See June Gruber/Raul Saucedo, Organic versus Artificial Thinking, in. John Brockmann, op. cit. p. 444.

for the death or immortality of "Homo Androidus"[50] not priests or shamans, but scientists and engineers will be responsible.[51]

Finally, first a conceptual clarification. Above was always spoken of the "singularity". Some readers who are familiar with natural science may have wondered what this astronomical "infinity" or the dissolution of space and time have to do with our text. Well, here we are talking about the so-called "technological singularity", which Kurzweil has defined as the point in time when AI surpasses human intelligence and thereby rapidly improves itself and makes new inventions, i.e. when "weak AI"[52] becomes strong or "Artificial Super Intelligence" (ASI) alias the "algorithmic upper class".[53]

Whether this step will only be the last invention of mankind[54] or even mean the end of mankind, as Stephen Hawking believed,[55] or whether mankind will not destroy itself beforehand, the author is not able to predict. But should we come to a peaceful symbiosis with the ASI, he holds it in the figurative sense with Zuse's quote: "The danger" that the computer becomes like man is not as great as the danger that man becomes like the computer.[56]

That may not be an enticing future. What is interesting is that the makers of AI, i.e. computer scientists and natural scientists, take the development as a given and are even already ranting about interstellar travel and the colonization of the universe as "quasi-aliens".[57] For them, emotions and flashes of inspiration, as the name actually suggests, are also just complex molecular-electronic firing. In contrast, the humanists consider their object of knowledge, the human mind or consciousness, soul, conscience or qualia, etc., to be something that AI can never approach.

The author, in the modesty incumbent upon him, will certainly not attempt to decide the eternal dispute between the metaphysical variant of "unconscious" consciousness such as the "idea of finite and thinking substance"[58] of Decartes, David Hume's " emotional ethics"[59] or Kant's "transcendental aesthetics"[60] in contrast to the natural scientific view

---

[50]Walter Simon, op. cit. p. 213.

[51]See Yuval Noah Harari, op. cit. p. 41.

[52]Yuval Noah, op. cit. p. 497.

[53]See Raymond Kurzweil, The Singularity Is Near. When Humans Transcend Biology. New York, 2005, p. 21 ff.

[54]See Nick Bostrum, op. cit. p. 50 ff.

[55]See, inter alia, Stephen Hwakings in BBC interview of 19.01.2016.

[56]Konrad Zuse, Good Quotes in: https://gutezitate.com/zitat/176576

[57]See inter alia Michio Haku, op. cit., p. 28 and p. 94 ff.

[58]See Andreas Kemmerling: Ideen des Ichs. Studies on Descartes' Philosophy, 2nd ed. Frankfurt am Main 2005.

[59]See Edward Craig: David Hume. An Introduction to his Philosophy, Frankfurt 1979.

[60]See Otfried Höffe: Immanuel Kant, 7th ed., Munich 2007.

such as Nietzsche's "subjective-perspective cognition"[61] or K. Popper with his "objective cognition".[62] In contrast to Decartes' "Cogito, ergo sum" the author only allows himself a **"Dubito**, ergo sum".

In order to pursue the question of what level of consciousness the ASI can reach, the author makes use of B. Pascal's "Theory of Bet"* as a paradigm.[63] If there is a "supernatural" consciousness or conscience, then it cannot program the ASI for itself, is the initially logical conclusion. But is this conclusion really final? If it is true for the ASI that it can evolve beyond human intelligence, then the bet is that it can also reach a level of cognition where a "supernatural" consciousness becomes possible for it. And to add to the wager: Even if it were to be proven that there are no such transcendent states of consciousness in human beings at all, in the distant future the ASI could cultivate itself into dimensions of cognition that made it "superhuman" with "consciousness".—If it doesn't happen, then we just speculated nicely and lost the bet without anyone getting hurt. And so below we come back to the comprehensible.

If consciousness is narrowed down only as a "state of mind in which one has knowledge of one's own existence and the existence of an environment", then even humanists should accept the prospect that ASI can reach that level. And in the case of emotions such as hate, love, or envy, the humanities arguments against a binary simulation of the same show a rather tautological character. When, for instance, Gelernter defines "happiness" as non-computable "because it is outside the universe of computations as the state of a physical object"[64] this may sound very erudite, but it remains epistemically without substance. Even if there may be very good reasons against ASI, as Zweig and other influencers very present in the media always admonish, the author, who keeps himself value-free,[65] sees no chance to stop this development on a global level.

However, should the local worrywarts actually succeed in cutting us off technically from AI research, the Europeans will become the aborigines of modern times, from whom the "transis" occasionally buy "analogue" tomatoes and potatoes for their occasional retro-parties in the "European Cultural Heritage Center" with antique coinage.

---

[61] See Friedrich Nietzsche, Hauptwerke: Menschliches-Allzumenschliches, Also sprach Zarathustra, Jenseits von Gut und Böse, Hamburg, 2013.

[62] See Karl Popper, Logik der Forschung. Zur Erkenntnistheorie der modernen Naturwissenschaft, 11th ed.

[63] * The bet in a nutshell: If I live according to God's laws, and he really exists, I have provided for a nice afterlife, if he doesn't exist, at least I have lived a decent life without having missed much.—So I live godly.

See Blaise Pascal, On Religion and Some Other Objects (Pensées), translated by Edwald Wasmuth, Heidelberg 1963.

[64] David Gelernter, op. cit. p. 13.

[65] Katharina Zweig, op. cit. p. 269.

Literature

Armbruster A (Hrsg) (2018) Künstliche Intelligenz für jedermann, Wie wir von schlauen Computern profitieren, Das Einsteigerbuch, 1. Aufl. Frankfurter Allgemeine Buch, Frankfurt am Main

Aurnhammer A, Martin D (eds) (2003) Mythos Pygmalion. Texte von Ovid bis John. Reclam, Leipzig

Bordini L (2016) Artificial intelligence for cultural heritage. Cambridge Scholars Publishing, Cambridge

Bostrum N (2014) Superintelligenz, Szenarien einer kommenden Revolution, Aus dem Englischen von Jan-Erik Strasser, 1. Aufl. Suhrkamp, Berlin

Böttinger E, zu Putlitz J (eds) (2019) Die Zukunft der Medizin, Disruptive revolutionieren Medizin und Gesundheit. Medizinisch Wissenschaftliche Verlagsgesellschaft, Berlin

Brauer G (2019) Die Bit-Revolution, Künstliche Intelligenz steuert uns alle in Wirtschaft, Politik und Gesellschaft. UVK Verlagsgesellschaft mbH, München

Brockman J (2017) Was sollen wir von Künstlicher Intelligenz halten? Aus dem Englischen von Jürgen Schröder. Fischer, Frankfurt am Main

Brynjolfsson E, Mcaffee A (2015) The Second Machine Age Wie die nächste digitale Revolution unser aller Leben verändern wird, 2. Aufl. Börsenbuchverlag, Kulmbach

Buxmann P, Schmidt H (2019) Künstliche Intelligenz, Mit Algorithmen zum wirtschaftlichen Erfolg. Springer Gabler, Berlin

Cornelius A (2019) Künstliche Intelligenz, Entwicklungen, Erfolgsfaktoren und Einsatzmöglichkeiten, 1. Aufl. Haufe TaschenGuide, Freiburg i. Breisgau

Danne S (2018) My Love Brand, So werden Kunden und Mitarbeiter zu ihren Besten Markenbotschaftern. Linde international, München

Daugherty PR, Wilson HJ (2018) Human + Machine, Künstliche Intelligenz und die Zukunft der Arbeit. dtv, München

De Miranda L (ed) (2019) Künstliche Intelligenz & Robotik in 30 Sekunden. Bielo Verlagsgesellschaft mbH Vilnius, Vilnius

Dengel A (ed) (2012) Semantische Technologien, Grundlagen – Konzepte – Anwendungen. Spektrum Akad. Verlag, Heidelberg

Domingos P (2015) The master algorithm: how the quest for the ultimate learning machine will remake our world. Basic Books, Member of the Perseus Books Group, New York

Eberl U (2016) Smarte Maschinen, Wie Künstliche Intelligenz unser Leben verändert. Carl Hanser, München

Ertel W (2016) Grundkurs Künstliche Intelligenz, Eine praxisorientierte Einführung, 4. Aufl. Springer Vieweg, Heidelberg

© Springer Fachmedien Wiesbaden GmbH, part of Springer Nature 2021

G. Cisek, *The Triumph of Artificial Intelligence*,

https://doi.org/10.1007/978-3-658-34896-0

Ford M (2016) Aufstieg der Roboter. Plassen, Kulmbach

Gelernter D (2016) Gezeiten des Geistes, Die Vermessung unseres Bewusstseins. Ullstein, Berlin

Gentsch P (2018) Künstliche Intelligenz für Sales, Marketing und Service, 1. Aufl. Springer Nature, Wiesbaden

Gläß R (2018) Künstliche Intelligenz im Handel. Springer Nature, Wiesbaden

Gloger B (2017) Scrum think big. Carl Hanser, München

Görz G, Schneeberger J, Schmid U (2014) Handbuch der Künstlichen Intelligenz, 5., überarb. u. akt. Aufl. de Gruyter, Oldenburg

Graig E, Hume D (1979) Eine Einführung in seine Philosophie. Vittorio Klostermann, Frankfurt am Main

Gröner S, Heinecke S (2019) Kollege KI, Künstliche Intelligenz verstehen und sinnvoll im Unternehmen einsetzen. Redline, München

Gruber M-C, Bung J, Ziemann S (Hrsg) (2015) Autonome Automaten, 2. Aufl. Trafo Wissenschaftsverlag, Berlin

Gumbrecht HU (2018) Weltgeist im Silicon Valley: Leben und Denken im Zukunftsmodus. NZZ Libro, Zürich

Harari YN (2019) Homo Deus – a brief history of tomorrow, 8. Aufl. C.H. Beck, München

Harbeck G (1966) Einführung in die formale Logik, 2. bericht. Aufl. Vieweg, Braunschweig

Hawkins J (2004) On intelligence, how a new understanding of the brain will lead to the creation of truly intelligent machines. Times Books, New York

Herger M (2020) Wenn Affen von Affen lernen, Wie künstliche Intelligenz uns erst richtig zum Menschen macht. Plassen, Kulmbach

Hillenbrand T (2020) Qube. Kiepenheuer & Witsch, Köln

Hölfe O (2007) Immanuel Kant, 7. Aufl. C.H. Beck, München

Holtdorf C (2019) Coburger live-forum. Coburger Live-Forum, Coburg

Huss R (2019) Künstliche Intelligenz, Robotik und Big Data in der Medizin. Springer, Berlin

Kaku M (2012) Physics of the future the inventions that will transform our lives. Penguin, London

Kaku M (2019) Abschied von der Erde, Die Zukunft der Menschheit, 1. Aufl. Rowohlt, Hamburg

Kaplan J (2017) Künstliche Intelligenz, Übersetzung aus dem Englischen von Guido Lenz, 1. Aufl. MITP Verlags-GmbH & Co. KG, Frechen

Keese C (2016) Silicon Germany, Wie wir die digitale Transformation schaffen, 1. Aufl. Albrecht Knaus, München

Kemmerling A (2005) Ideen des Ichs, Studien zu Decartes' Philosophie, 2. Aufl. Vittorio Klostermann, Frankfurt am Main

Köhler-Schute C (2015) Industrie 4.0: Ein praxisorientierter Ansatz. KS-Energy-Verlag, Berlin

Kurzweil R (1993) KI, Das Zeitalter der künstlichen Intelligenz. Carl Hanser, München/Wien

Kurzweil R (2005) The singularity is near. When humans transcend biology. Penguin Group, New York

Kurzweil R (2012) How to create a mind, the secret of human thought revealed. Duckworth Overlook, New York

Lenzen M (2018) Künstliche Intelligenz, Was sie kann und was uns erwartet, 2. Aufl. C.H. Beck, München

Lenzen M (2020) Künstliche Intelligenz, Fakten, Chancen, Risiken. C.H. Beck, München

Lucks K (2020) Der Wettlauf um die Digitalisierung. Schäffer Poeschel, Stuttgart

Mainzer K (2003) KI – Künstliche Intelligenz, Grundlagen intelligenter Systeme. Primus, Darmstadt

Marr B (2020) Künstliche Intelligenz in Unternehmen, Innovative Anwendungen in 50 erfolgreichen Firmen. Wiley-VCH, Weinheim

Maté C (2020) Medizin ohne Ärzte, Ersetzt künstliche Intelligenz die menschliche Heilkunst? Residenz, Salzburg/Wien

Mayer-Schönberger V, Cukier K (2013) Big Data, Die Revolution, die unser Leben verändern wird, Übersetzung aus dem Englischen von Dagmar Mallett, 2. Aufl. Redline, München

Morozov E (2013) Smarte Neue Welt, Digitale Technik und die Freiheit des Menschen, 1. Aufl. Karl Blessing, München

Nassehi A (2019) Muster, Theorie der digitalen Gesellschaft, 2. Aufl. C.H. Beck, München

Nietzsche F (2013) Hauptwerke: Menschliches-Allzumenschliches, Also sprach Zarathustra, Jenseits von Gut und Böse. Nikol, Hamburg

Otte R (2019) Künstliche Intelligenz für Dummies, 1. Aufl. Wiley-VCH, Leipzig

Pascal B (1963) Über die Religion und einige andere Gegenstände (Pensées), Übersetzt von Edwald Wasmuth. Schneider, Heidelberg

Precht RD (2020) Künstliche Intelligenz und der Sinn des Lebens. Wilhelm Goldmann, München

Ramge T (2018) Mensch und Maschine, Wie Künstliche Intelligenz und Roboter unser Leben verändern, 2. Aufl. Reclam, Leipzig

Reinhart G (2017) Handbuch Industrie 4.0. Springer Vieweg, München

Riguzzi F (2018) Foundations of probabilistic logic programming, languages, semantics, inference and learning. River Publishers, Gistrup

Schulz T (Hrsg) (2017) Industrie 4.0, Potenziale erkennen und umsetzen, 1. Aufl. Vogel Business Media, Würzburg

Searle JR (1980) Minds, brains, and programs. In: The behavioral and brain sciences. Cambridge University Press, Berkeley

Simon W (2019) Künstliche Intelligenz, Was man wissen muss. Norderstedt. Leben 3.0, Mensch sein im Zeitalter Künstlicher Intelligenz. Books on Demand, Berlin

Spreen D (2000) Cyborgs und andere Technokörper, Ein Essay im Grenzbereich zwischen Bios und Techne, 2. Aufl. Erster Deutscher Fantasy Club, Passau

Syska A, Lievre P (2016) Illusion 4.0, Deutschlands naiver Traum von der smarten Fabrik. CETPM Publishing, Herrieden

Tegmark M (2017) Leben 3.0, Mensch sein im Zeitalter Künstlicher Intelligenz. Ullstein, Berlin

Topol E (2020) Deep Medicine, Wie KI das Gesundheitswesen menschlicher macht. mitp Verlags GmbH, Frechen

Volkens B, Anderson K (2018) Digital Human, Der Mensch im Mittelpunkt der Digitalisierung. Campus, Frankfurt am Main

Volland H (2018) Die Kreative Macht der Maschinen, 1. Aufl. Beltz, Weinheim

Wagener A (2019) Künstliche Intelligenz im Marketing – ein Crashkurs, 1. Aufl. Haufe, Freiburg/München/Stuttgart

Walsh T (2019) 2062, Das Jahr, in dem die Künstliche Intelligenz uns ebenbürtig sein wird, 1. Aufl. Riva, München

Wärter J (2019) Crowdwork. ÖGB, Wien

Weizenbaum J (1977) Die Macht der Computer und die Ohnmacht der Vernunft, 2. Aufl. Suhrkamp, Frankfurt am Main

Žižek S (2020) Hegel im verdrahteten Gehirn. S. Fischer, Frankfurt am Main

Zukunftsinstitut GH (ed) (2019) Künstliche Intelligenz, Wie wir KI als Zukunftstechnologie produktiv nutzen können. Zukunftsinstitut, Frankfurt am Main

Zweig K (2019) Ein Algorithmus hat kein Taktgefühl, Wo künstliche Intelligenz sich irrt, warum es uns betrifft und was wir dagegen tun können, 3. Aufl. Heyne, München

Index

© Springer Fachmedien Wiesbaden GmbH, part of Springer Nature 2021
G. Cisek, *The Triumph of Artificial Intelligence*,
https://doi.org/10.1007/978-3-658-34896-0